"Peace is imperative in a world where ethnic, religious, and political divisions between people are intensifying. But it's only us, as Christ-followers, who can demonstrate the radical love of our Savior and facilitate true and lasting peace—a state of shalom. Jon Huckins and Jer Swigart have provided a timely manual for engaging in the gritty, risky work we're called to when we sign on to build God's kingdom 'on earth as it is in heaven.'"

Rich Stearns, president, World Vision

"Jon and Jer are called not only to be peacemakers individually but to holistically change the church's understanding and practice of this task. They have put their rich wisdom and experience into this practical, relevant, and timely book that weaves theological insights, personal stories, and practical applications into a comprehensive manual for everyday peacemaking. They remind us that everyday peacemaking is not a side activity of our Christian lives, but core to our walk as disciples of Christ. Through this book, they teach us to lean into conflict with humility and grace, and to move toward the difficult task of building relationships with those on the margins of society who are often our best teachers. At a time when conflict is so easy to instigate and arguments are so easily had, they point to the better way of peace that reflects the power of a broken and resurrected Christ. What would it look like for the church to take seriously its call to bring about peace in a broken and hurting world? This book provides the way!"

Jenny Yang, vice president of advocacy and policy, World Relief, coauthor of *Welcoming the Stranger*

"Jesus' infectious peacemaking has taken hold of Jer Swigart and Jon Huckins. This book explains how and why—but even more, how and why they passionately want it to happen in the lives of any who are followers of Jesus. In a world of broken trust, hostile prejudice, religious violence, and pervasive fear, our world desperately needs God's people to be humble, courageous, and just peacemakers. The need for this fruit of the Spirit could hardly be more urgent."

Mark Labberton, president, Fuller Theological Seminary

"What if Christians believed they were the reconciled beloved? If we believed we were worthy of God's own Son who came to reconcile himself to us, we might believe that peacemaking and reconciliation were not just important to God but the heart of God. I was convicted that I can and must do more.

Huckins and Swigart make peacemaking real and doable in a world filled with conflict—from families to continents. The theological basis draws the reader deeply into Scripture. The stories woven throughout the book put faces on why peacemaking is an imperative. This book will be invaluable to an adult Sunday school class or as an additional text in a college classroom."

Shirley Hoogstra, president, Council for Christian Colleges and Universities

"In a world ravaged by violence and in a country that is the epicenter of global violence and the arms trade, the work that Jon and Jer are doing to disarm hearts, heal our streets, and reimagine the world is some of the most important stuff happening on the planet. The Global Immersion Project and this book capture the heart of Jesus and cast a vision for a world we can be proud to leave our children."

Shane Claiborne, author, activist, peacemaker

"I've learned so much about peacemaking and about what it means to be a neighbor from Jon and Jer, and I'm thrilled that so many people will get to learn from them through this timely and essential book. I'll be handing it out left and right because I can't think of very many things more necessary for our communities and our world right now."

Shauna Niequist, author of *Present Over Perfect*

"This is evangelical Christianity at its best: two young Christian friends, devoted to Christ, rooted in Scripture, following Jesus in new directions, utterly unafraid to go where faithful discipleship requires. This road map to the contemporary practice of Christian peacemaking is an extraordinarily practical and inspiring guide for all of us."

David Gushee, professor of Christian ethics, Mercer University, author of *Kingdom Ethics* and *Changing Our Mind*

"At a time when our world is dominated by stories of indifference and injustice, I'm excited to recommend Jon and Jer's new book, *Mending the Divides*, which is full of with hope-filled stories that will inspire you to not give up dreaming and to work for the world God desires for us all."

Noel Castellanos, president, CCDA, author of *Where the Cross Meets the Street*

"There are a host of Christian books emerging about God's call to justice. *Mending the Divides* is the only book I have seen that outlines the relationship between justice and peacemaking on multiple levels, from the spiritual foundation to the practical steps we all need to take. If you take nothing else from this book, the stories from the frontlines of shalom could change your life. I am thankful for and encouraged by Jon and Jer's gift to us all."

Alexia Salvatierra, coauthor of *Faith-Rooted Organizing*

"One of the most compelling ways followers of Jesus can put the unique beauty of God's kingdom on display is by serving as peacemakers in the midst of conflict. Unfortunately, few Christians have been taught how to do this in their everyday lives. Nor have they ever been shown why doing so is a matter of urgency. This is why this deeply personal, theologically insightful, and immensely practical book is such an important gift to the church. I wish every believer would read this book, for I can guarantee them that they won't finish this book unchanged!"

Greg Boyd, pastor, Woodland Hills Church, author of *Is God to Blame?* and *Letters from a Skeptic*

"This book is a call to remember that our faith is not in a warlord but in a slaughtered lamb. It is a call to embody the very nature of God, whose essence is shalom. Far from being an escapist flight into the heavenly hereafter, Jon and Jer direct our attention to the practice of what they call 'everyday peacemaking.' God has launched a 'scandalous and costly' restoration campaign. And he has asked us to join in the ranks—not just in the hereafter, but in the here and now, in conflicted families and fractured communities. Carefully, humbly, and compellingly, *Mending the Divides* gives us the tools we need for such a time as this—gently and insistently taking our gaze and our affection back to Jesus, who revealed that peace isn't a destination but a way of life."

Laura Truax, author of *Love Let Go* and *Undone*

"Yes and amen! *Mending the Divides* is the gospel of peace made practical by brothers seeking to live it. It makes clear that Christian peacemaking requires a cross and trusts in resurrection. May the church learn to live this book!"

Jarrod McKenna, national advisor on faith and activism, World Vision Australia, pastor of Westcity Church

JON HUCKINS | *JER SWIGART*

MENDING THE DIVIDES

FOREWORD BY
LYNNE HYBELS

CREATIVE

LOVE IN A

CONFLICTED

WORLD

IVP Books
An imprint of InterVarsity Press
Downers Grove, Illinois

InterVarsity Press
P.O. Box 1400, Downers Grove, IL 60515-1426
ivpress.com
email@ivpress.com

*InterVarsity Press® is the book-publishing division of InterVarsity Christian Fellowship/USA®, a movement
of students and faculty active on campus at hundreds of universities, colleges, and schools of nursing in the
United States of America, and a member movement of the International Fellowship of Evangelical Students.
For information about local and regional activities, visit intervarsity.org.*

*All Scripture quotations, unless otherwise indicated, are taken from The Holy Bible, New International
Version®, NIV®. Copyright © 1973, 1978, 1984, 2011 by Biblica, Inc.™ Used by permission of Zondervan.
All rights reserved worldwide. www.zondervan.com. The "NIV" and "New International Version" are
trademarks registered in the United States Patent and Trademark Office by Biblica, Inc.™*

*While any stories in this book are true, some names and identifying information may have been
changed to protect the privacy of individuals.*

Published in association with the literary agency of Mark Oestreicher.

Cover design: David Fassett
Interior design: Daniel van Loon
Images: abstract: © Mina De La O/Getty Images
      blue dust: © Carther/iStockphoto
ISBN 978-0-8308-4484-5 (print)
ISBN 978-0-8308-8110-9 (digital)

Printed in the United States of America ∞

Library of Congress Cataloging-in-Publication Data

A catalog record for this book is available from the Library of Congress.

P   25   24   23   22   21   20   19   18   17   16   15   14   13   12   11   10   9   8   7   6   5   4   3   2   1
Y   36   35   34   33   32   31   30   29   28   27   26   25   24   23   22   21   20   19   18   17

Dedicated to our kids, Ava, Ruby,

Rosie, Andrs, Lou, Hank, and Soren.

May you become the next generation

of everyday peacemakers who join

God in mending our divided world.

CONTENTS

FOREWORD

Lynne Hybels

I was in northern Iraq, in the home of a Muslim sheik. My two North American friends and I had been invited to share a meal with a dozen Muslim clerics. As we sat in a huge circle on the floor, hands deep into a feast of juicy chicken, seasoned rice, and brilliantly colored salads, our new friends poured out their hearts about the suffering of their country.

"Please tell Americans that ISIS does not represent us."

"Our people—men, women, and children—are being ruthlessly murdered."

"Here, take these prayer beads. Please join us in praying for peace."

Silently, I turned my face back and forth from speaker to translator, tears brimming.

After dinner, we sipped sweet mint tea as our host moved from the litany of despair to the poetry of hope. With eyes closed, the sheik began to sing, softly at first, but quickly building to a crescendo of joy. People began to smile, then laugh. New friends! Heartfelt conversation! A shared commitment to a better future! A vision of peace!

I fingered the prayer beads and slowly scanned the room. Was this really happening? And more to the point, how did a small-town Michigan girl end up in war-torn Iraq listening to a roomful of Muslim clerics and a singing sheik?

The truth is, it wasn't my first time in a war zone. In the early 1990s, as the former Yugoslavia crumbled amidst a series of horrific wars, I visited a medical center in Croatia where devastated civilians stared into space like zombies. In Bosnia I met children so traumatized from watching their parents murdered that they sat all day in school silently chewing their fingernails or drawing pictures of death.

Years later in the Democratic Republic of Congo I met with women brutally raped by rebel soldiers who concluded it was cheaper—and more effective—to rape a woman than waste a bullet on killing her. Rape enough women, they reasoned, and you can destroy the soul of an entire village.

Later still I was challenged by Middle Eastern Christians to better understand the deadly conflict between Israelis and Palestinians. So I traveled to the Holy Land repeatedly, listening and learning. From there I went on to visit Jordan, Lebanon, and Iraq, where millions fleeing the violence of war crossed country borders in the dark of night with bullets chasing them.

At the time, each of these trips seemed like a one-off—singular and unrelated responses to unexpected invitations. Only in retrospect did the pattern of my travels become clear.

I am convinced I was divinely led from conflict to conflict for two simple reasons: (1) to see up close the horrific repercussions of un-checked conflict, and (2) to learn from heroic, honest-to-goodness peacemakers. These two lessons—along with the words in our own Scriptures that call us to peace—convinced me that peacemaking is a vital part of Christian discipleship.

And now here I am, a lot older and a little wiser. While I still feel an undeniable call to conflict zones, I've discovered I don't always have to travel far to find one. The lessons I learned on foreign soils have challenged me to give greater attention to escalating conflicts much closer to home.

Sadly, I live in a country that feels increasingly polarized into divisive factions, even at war with itself. A country where increasing numbers of residents are seen and treated as the frightening "other." A country where public discourse routinely devolves into hateful, soul-shaming words. A country desperately in need of grassroots peacemakers—ordinary people offering words of love around every dinner table, showing up at places of pain in every neighborhood, scattered broadly throughout every church congregation, gently speaking up on every social media site, earnestly seeking divine wisdom as they speak truth to power.

One of the blessings of my meandering journey across conflict zones was meeting Jon Huckins and Jer Swigart. They had learned from many of the same global peacemakers I'd encountered, and they were articulating those lessons in a way that applied every day and everywhere—from private interpersonal disagreements to deadly international conflicts.

I couldn't help but ask, "Do you guys have these teachings written down somewhere?"

I'm sure I'm not the only person who asked that question, but I had the pleasure of being one of the first to read the finished product. And I love every word! This book is theologically compelling, richly personal, and intensely practical. And I can guarantee this: If you read it with an open heart, you will be transformed. You'll have new eyes to see the humanity, dignity, and image of God in everyone. And you'll be eager to join the growing army of peacemakers who—to quote Jon and Jer—are "building uncommon friendships" and "getting creative in love."

Together, let's accept the challenges issued so brilliantly by these two young peacemakers. Let's mend the divisions we face personally and build bridges of understanding to those who are different from us. In so doing, we'll be following in the way of Jesus and furthering the healing work of God in this beautiful but broken world.

ONE

CONFUSED, DIVIDED, AND PARALYZED

Not long ago we were on a video call with a young couple from the Midwest. They were business owners, influencers in their city, and leaders in their church. They had recently completed a three-month course with their faith community called "The Mission of God."

As we listened to their experience unfold, we noticed that they kept referring to the elusive "one day" when they would join God on mission. Concepts like "getting our house in order" and mission "over there" crept into the conversation, causing us to wonder what they had discovered about the what, where, who, and how of God's mission. And so, finally, we paused the conversation with a question:

"What *is* the mission of God?"

They stared at us. We stared back, waiting for them to wax eloquent about the very topic they had just given three months of study to.

Silence.

Finally he said something about "love" and then, after a nervous laugh, admitted, "I . . . I guess we're not sure."

Not long ago, "We're not sure" was our response as well when asked about the mission of God. We knew we were supposed to "follow Jesus" and "save lost souls" and "love God and love people," but if you really pushed us, we were confused about who God was, what God actually did in Jesus, and who God did "it" for.

The ramifications of this mission confusion were significant for us. Rather than engaging every day with clarity about our part in God's mission, we meandered through the landscape of a violent world, disturbed by the interpersonal, local, and international conflicts that were tearing our world apart. We imagined that Jesus had something to say about the pain of broken relationships, broken systems, and broken lives, and we anticipated that God would eventually do something about it. We longed to follow God in ways that were helpful, but because we weren't sure how to do that, we simply hung on to a moral existence. We hoped that the conflicts raging around us would resolve themselves and that if we lived well enough we'd go to heaven when we died. From our limited theological and cultural perspective, God was singularly concerned with the redemption of the human souls. So we and our churches were too.

And then everything changed. For both of us.

JON

My wife, Jan, was seven months pregnant with our first child and we figured we should go on one more adventure before the new adventure of parenting got underway. As a pastor, seminary student, and academic nut, my dream was to go to Israel and study the Scriptures while walking through the historical contexts of Jesus. The dream came true and from the moment we stepped off the plane in Tel Aviv, I was filled with wonder like a kid on Christmas morning.

We stayed in the Christian Quarter of the Old City of Jerusalem and woke up to the sound of the call to prayer that was both beautiful and mystical as it echoed through the narrow streets. Each day would involve "field trips" to biblical locations like Jericho, Bethlehem, Hebron, and Masada. I was in heaven, soaking up every piece of information and new experience.

Before we headed out for the daily pilgrimage, we would go through the breakfast line in the hotel and interact casually with the restaurant staff. We were especially drawn to one man, who one morning asked my wife the bold question, "How far along are you?"

"Seven months," she responded.

He broke into a smile from ear to ear and said, "My wife is too!" His name was Milad.

In that moment something shifted between us as we moved from acquaintances living on opposite sides of the world to parents who were about to embark on a life-changing adventure. From that point on our conversations deepened and our time with Milad became a highlight of the day. One morning he pulled me aside after I finished breakfast and said, "I get off work late tonight. Do you want to meet me on the roof for a drink and conversation?" I immediately said yes.

Little did I know saying yes would change my life forever.

As we stood on the roof overlooking Herod's Palace, the Dome of the Rock, the Mount of Olives, and all of the Old City, we had a casual conversation about the World Cup, parenting fears, and our families. Then his cadence began to slow. He turned to me somberly and asked, "Why do your people think I'm a terrorist?"

I was so shocked I just squeaked, "Excuse me?"

"I'm an Arab Christian Palestinian who lives in the West Bank. I love Jesus just like you do. He is my Messiah! My village, Bethany, is just on the other side of the Mount of Olives and is the place where Jesus raised Lazarus to life. How can you American Christians pray for your meals each morning and go look at all your holy sites when just five minutes away your brothers and sisters in Christ are experiencing daily oppression and occupation?"

I was paralyzed.

My worldview had blown up and my heart had broken. I didn't understand all of what Milad was saying, but I knew I was changed forever in that moment. He went on to tell me that the reason he served food and cleaned rooms at the hotel was to make enough money to run a nonprofit organization in his village that taught reconciliation to children surrounded by violence.

Going and studying two-thousand-year-old stones that Jesus may or may not have walked on was no longer interesting to me. I wanted to see and experience the way Jesus was presently alive and at work through the life of my friend Milad and his wife, Manar. From that point on my wife and I would cut out of class early, jump on the next public bus crossing through military checkpoints into the West Bank, and spend time with our new friends in Bethany.

What we saw in the lives of Milad and Manar was nothing short of the resurrection Jesus had enacted in the same village two thousand years before. As they walked the streets, kids from all around the village would pour out of their homes to follow them to the "House of Hope." The space was a busted-out second-story apartment and their infrastructure consisted solely of an archaic laptop, but the glow on the children's faces turned it into the most magical and beautiful place on earth.

We were finally experiencing the Holy Land, and it looked nothing like we had anticipated. Our time with Milad and Manar led me to begin asking some of the hardest questions I had ever faced—the questions that would launch me into this wild ride of peacemaking.

As a seminary-trained pastor, how could I have been so blind to and complicit in the suffering of my Palestinian brothers and sisters? What theology and politics had I inherited that allowed me to demonize—or at the very least turn a blind eye to—an entire people group? What other blind spots was I unaware of because I hadn't been given the tools to see the way Jesus saw? Why was the church contributing to violence rather than reconciliation? If the church was being used as a pawn of violence in the life of my friend Milad, what might happen if that same energy was used to be an instrument of peace in Milad's life and our world in general?

From that point on I gave my life to seeking and living into the answers to those questions.

JER

In October of 2005 I read a front-page article about a 7.2-magnitude earthquake that had just ravaged the tribal villages of Northern Pakistan. At the time I had no idea where Pakistan was on the globe. Not only did I not have any Pakistani friends, I knew zero Muslims. Just four years removed from 9/11, all I "knew" about Pakistan was that it was enemy territory, that Osama bin Laden, public enemy number one, was believed to be hiding there, and that the Arab Muslims of that land were dangerous terrorists.

As I read the article about the thousands who had perished and the three million who were now homeless in the Himalayas, something broke open inside of me. Two phone calls with mentors later, I had a connection into Pakistan and the funding to make it happen. A month later I landed at the militarized Islamabad airport and was immediately shuttled eight hours north to a United Nations helipad. I boarded my first helicopter ever and, within ten hours of being in the country, found myself on top of the Himalayas at the epicenter of the earthquake, among the tribal villages of Northern Pakistan, mere kilometers away from the Tora Bora caves.

Because I had a notebook in hand when I arrived, the job assigned me by Mumtaz, the presiding Pakistani general, was to be the communications liaison between the villages, the Pakistani military, and the United Nations. Over the next three weeks Mumtaz and I listened to the requests of 157 sets of village elders who were mourning the devastation caused by the earthquake. I in turn negotiated with the UN to ensure that the necessary supplies were delivered.

In the Pakistani village of Jabba and in the context of friendship with the "enemy," my understanding of who God is, where God is, whose side God is on, and what God is up to in the world was upended. My experience of intentional displacement within "enemy territory" was causing a very necessary renovation of my theology.

The crisis of my conversion occurred on my last day in Jabba. A final set of elders made their way into the village. But this time the Russian-era machine guns were not hanging at their sides; they were drawn and pointing at those of us sitting around the fire. Immediately my new friends raised their guns in return. Guns were now pointing at faces and every person involved was screaming. The chaos was suffocating.

Slowly Mumtaz was able to de-escalate the situation and the visiting elders were invited, still at gunpoint, to our fire. A four-hour conversation ensued through which I began to understand the reason for the violent tension: these two tribes had been at civil war for over thirty years. As Jabba was the only village with enough clearance for helicopters to land, the visiting elders knew that the only way their people would make it through the winter was if they brokered peace with their enemy. Mumtaz looked at me and, with more urgency in his voice than I had experienced in our three weeks together, said, "I need you to write a peace treaty."

Now let's be honest. I was a Midwestern-born-and-raised young white pastor from the San Francisco Bay Area. Nothing in my life had prepared me for the three weeks I had already spent in Jabba, much less for drafting a peace treaty between warring Pakistani tribes. But I had a notebook and a pen in my hands, and I had an understanding of the agreements being made. I had earned the trust of the Pakistani general, the elders of Jabba, and the UN commander. Apparently Mumtaz thought I had everything I needed, so I began to write. After a couple rounds of edits, each of the presiding elders signed the treaty, as did Mumtaz, the UN commander, and I.

As I watched the visiting elders being escorted out of Jabba, no longer at gunpoint, the gospel became clearer to me than it had ever been before. In Jesus, God had waged a decisive peace that worked, and it meant that people who weren't going to survive would now flourish. As I looked down at the peace treaty in my notebook, mission also became crystal clear: as a follower of Jesus, I had just joined God in making peace real in the world. I realized in that moment that while the redemption of the human soul was in God's peacemaking focus, so was the restoration of interpersonal relationships, broken systems, and global conflicts.

Peace wasn't only of value to God; it's central to who God is.

Peacemaking wasn't one of God's peripheral practices; it's God's mission.

Could it be that peacemaking is central to what it means to follow Jesus?

OUR STORIES MERGED

Both of us were being formed by God in beautifully bizarre corners of our global village. With newfound clarity on the gospel of peace and the mission of peacemaking, we each returned to the United States with a lot to learn about living every day as Jesus-following peacemaking practitioners.

Our learning was experiential—we found our lives intersecting more and more with the painful divides in our families, neighborhoods, and cities—and it was also traditional; we were enrolled as students at Fuller Theological Seminary, Jer in Northern California and Jon in Southern California. Unbeknownst to the other, we each spent as much of our learning as possible focusing on the biblical concepts of peace, justice, and reconciliation. Our experiential and traditional learning fused near the end of our coursework when we both traveled to Israel-Palestine to study peacemaking under the instruction of the late Dr. Glen Stassen.

It was there that our stories collided.

The conflict was our classroom, but it was our instructors who captured our attention. While we had studied peacemaking and even practiced it in our own contexts, we had never met peacemakers like these: men and women whose faith in Jesus compelled them to spend their lives in costly and creative ways so that the severed divides between their peoples could be mended.

Throughout those two weeks we started asking a set of questions:

- What is peace?
- Who is a peacemaker?
- Are there practices of peacemaking? And if so, what are they and where would we find them?

- Where does peacemaking happen?
- How would we train the people in our churches in the way of peace?
- What would be different in the world if North American Christians understood peacemaking as central to following Jesus?

These questions were the genesis of the Global Immersion Project. Today, Global Immersion is a leading peacemaking training organization that is activating the North American church as an instrument of peace in our world. Through our immersive trainings, peacemaking is becoming reintergrated into the North American church's understanding of who God is, what God did in Jesus, what God is doing now, and what role we get to play in it.

In the chapters to follow, you're going to learn about the journey we took as individuals, local practitioners, and faith leaders into the peacemaking heart and mission of God. As we go, you'll discover the theological odyssey we had to take and you'll meet some of our friends, mentors, and heroes who are faith-based peacemaking practitioners within the contexts of their own homes, neighborhoods, cities, and countries. Ultimately, throughout this book you're going to discover a big God with an expansive, restorative wingspan who invites us to join in ushering in the new world God is making.

THREE DISCLAIMERS

By now you might have some questions. What does peacemaking really have to do with the Christian faith? Isn't this more a conversation for activists, humanitarians, politicians, and the United Nations than for the church? With the stories of violence, armed conflict, broken relationships, and systemic injustice that saturate our social media feeds, isn't peacemaking unrealistic at best and a colossal waste of time at worst?

Don't worry; ten years ago we were asking the exact same questions. As far as we were concerned, peacemaking was about the political activism of idealistic noninfluencers on the fringes of society.

As you're soon to discover, we were dead wrong. But before we head into the fray, we want to offer three important disclaimers. You see, as we continue our personal journeys of following Jesus in today's world, we are humbled by how many blind spots we have based on our limited worldview as white, straight, male, Christian leaders living in the United States. Because we know shining light on these blind spots is critical to our formation and faithfulness to the one we follow, we have individually and collectively invited a diverse network of friends, mentors, and guides to accompany us along the path. In other words, we have handed them a flashlight and asked them to expose the stuff remaining in the dark. While we acknowledge blind spots that still need revealing, here are a few things we want to own up front.

First, we don't believe God is male or female but genderful. In other words, both females and males are image-bearers of a God who both encompasses and transcends gender. Because Scripture was written and compiled in a patriarchal culture, most of its authors were male and the majority of pronouns used to describe God are male ... although, thankfully, not all! We think language matters and we in no way want to diminish the male or female characteristics of God. For the most part we use gender-neutral pronouns for God, but not completely. We acknowledge that our language falls short of the full characteristics of God and also want to acknowledge the equality of women and men from creation to the present.

We also write from the unique vantage point of being middle-class white men in the United States. At times this worldview will omit an important perspective and vantage point that we should not only consider but value. We apologize in advance for ways our cultural blind spots may be exposed as a result. That said, we have spent our lives working to learn from minority voices in the majority world as a way to help us better understand the beautiful complexity and contribution of people from a variety of racial, geographic, religious, political, and economic contexts.

Finally, we want to be up front about the fact that we see a distinction between peacemaking and justice. We see justice as a critical and nonnegotiable element of peacemaking that has to be pursued if we are to embrace a holistic understanding of God's work in the world and our central part in participating in God's mission of peacemaking. We will zero in on a variety of definitions, perspectives, and practices of justice in chapter seven when we outline our third everyday peacemaking practice, *contend*. With that said, we'd encourage you to engage the content of this book not solely through the lens of a "justice genre" but through a whole new framework of life and discipleship we call *everyday peacemaking*.

JOINING THE MOVEMENT

Although the glowing ember of peace continues to build into a flame, our world is still experiencing pain, trauma, and division. In the moment we celebrate our relative peace, someone in our home, on our street, or on the other side of the world is navigating the high seas of interpersonal, local, or international conflict.

The stakes are high.

In the last few years we have heard many stories of conflict, from broken identities to broken interpersonal relationships.

The stories have spanned local systemic injustice all the way to global conflict.

Sarah grew up the daughter of a powerful father and an insecure mother. Dad spoiled her while mom ignored her. Despite her endless attempts, she could never attain the attention and affection she craved from her parents, so she searched elsewhere to find both. Over time she learned how to thrive through disintegration. On the outside she was a Christian overachiever while behind closed doors she was dangerously experimental. While others saw her as the epitome of success, she understood herself to be a fractured, lonely failure. When she turned eighteen, she bought a one-way ticket to San Francisco, caught a cab to the Golden Gate Bridge, took in the unspeakable beauty around her, climbed over the rail, and jumped.

Michael grew up in a rough, impoverished, lower-class neighborhood. His father was incarcerated and his mother did everything she could to help him and his three siblings succeed. He beat the odds and graduated from high school, taking extra coursework to qualify for college. So proud was his mother of her college-accepted son that she encouraged him to soak up the summer with his friends doing what they loved most: writing and recording rap lyrics that expressed their experiences of growing up black in America. And then there was an altercation with a white police officer that left him shot multiple times and bleeding to death in the sun-baked streets of Ferguson, Missouri.

Stephanie married the love of her life. Together she and her husband raised their daughter and created space for foster children to have a semblance of home. And then her husband started disappearing. One night turned into one week and then one month. He would always return, she would take him back, and life would seemingly return to normal. But the time he was gone for three months, things changed in the neighborhood. Late at night strange cars with unfamiliar people started showing up at her home. She would let them in, but only for a short time. Police presence increased and she grew distant from friends and neighbors. She was burdened and shamed by their heavy stares and whispers but felt she had no other choice than to hide behind locked doors that opened only for the exchange of the money she so desperately needed. She needed to put food on the table for her kids. Sex and meth were the quickest ways to do it.

Gloria spent her young life surviving the violence of Guatemalan drug lords, gang wars, and extreme poverty. Her grandmother was painfully aware that her granddaughter's future in Central America carried the inevitable threats of rape, prostitution, and death. So grandma made an unthinkable decision: she gathered what little she had and sent her teenage granddaughter, alone, on one of the most dangerous migrations in the world. This young, beautiful, innocent girl risked her life and had her innocence stripped from her on the tops of freight trains so that she could have a shot at a safer, more livable future in the United States. Tragically, she never made it. Along the way Gloria was kidnapped, gang raped, trafficked, and enslaved in the red light district of Tijuana where she was sold over and over again to satisfy the appetites of lonely men.

Contemporary stories of pain, conflict, broken identity, severed relationships, injustice, and revenge could fill the shelves of countless libraries. Sadly, many of us remain oblivious, indifferent, or paralyzed by the realities experienced by many in our homes, neighborhoods, cities, country, and world.

But God's mission is the redemption of all things—broken lives, broken relationships, and broken systems. The good news is that, embedded throughout the country and world, men and women are refusing to simply sit with the hard questions, lament, and pray for healing. Instead they are committed to becoming the answers to their prayers by actively joining God in the work of restoration.

As we work with individuals and churches across the United States and the world, we are inspired and fueled by the lives of Jesus-followers who are taking this peacemaking way of life seriously. From small-town streets and remote villages to bustling urban centers, the everyday peacemaking movement isn't just beginning. It is already well underway.

> Bri and Adam sat in our one of our peacemaking workshops visibly coming alive as the story of Jesus' movement toward the other in pursuit of loving his enemies captured their minds and hearts and began to stir their actions. Soon after, they leveraged their privilege by choosing a countercultural life of downward mobilization and moving into a low-income neighborhood in Des Moines, Iowa. They began to immerse themselves in the lives and stories of their neighbors not as a project, but as a way of life. Their home is now a space to host new friends—most of whom don't look like them—and is a signpost of the healing God has in mind for all humanity.
>
> Steve is the pastor of a majority white congregation in the suburbs of Minneapolis. After going to Israel-Palestine with us to learn from our Jewish, Muslim, and Christian friends working for peace, he discovered that everyday

peacemaking isn't an add-on to his faith but the very embodiment of it. He embraced peacemaking knowing that moving toward the other and loving his "enemies" could cost him his reputation and even his life. Upon arriving back home, he created space for his community to identify who they considered "the other" or "the enemy" in their own city. It was a process both of confession and awakening. A couple of months later, Philando Castile, an unarmed black man, was killed by police. Rather than sit on the sidelines paralyzed by fear, misunderstanding, or apathy, the community was on the front lines of lamenting the tragedy with their friends of color and calling for restoration on the streets of Minneapolis.

Diane is a middle-aged woman who lives in Phoenix with a heart for walking alongside those in pain and suffering, but she wasn't sure where her gifts could tangibly meet the needs of her neighbors. Knowing very little about Muslims or the plight of refugees, she discovered that her city was full of families who had fled violence in Africa and the Middle East and were now trying to make a home in Phoenix. So in 2011, Diane and others founded a multifaith community that intentionally creates opportunities where women of different faiths can gather together, meet "the other" in a safe environment, and break down the walls of fear through events such as service projects, book clubs, and prayer events.

We were recently with our friend and mentor Daoud Nasser, a Palestinian Christian whose family chooses the way of peace fueled by the message "We refuse to be enemies." Having shared his story of peacemaking in the Holy Land, he closed by saying, "The world will be a different place when North American Christians follow the Jesus they talk about."

We agree. And every day we are given more reason to believe it to be true as Christians choose cross-shaped lives and take seriously their call to follow an enemy-loving God. This is the new world God is making and we all get to be part of it.

This book is designed to equip you to live a similar story and be a partner in the movement.

REFLECT AND DISCUSS

1. Before reading this chapter, how did you define the mission of God? What did participation with God in that mission look and sound like?

2. What are your perceptions and misperceptions of peacemaking? How have you been a part of restoration in simple and profound ways?

3. What is the interpersonal conflict, local injustice, or global conflict you currently find yourself within or compelled toward?

TWO

SPEAKING OF PEACE

At the very beginning of the Global Immersion story, we sat with one of our advisors on a porch overlooking the Rocky Mountains. Rick Malouf is a gentle soul with an edgy, strategic curiosity that makes everything and everyone around him better. We had been in conversation for nearly an hour about peace and reconciliation. Playing devil's advocate, he questioned our every thought about peace, what it required, what it looked like, whether it was the same as justice or something far more.

The conversation, equal parts exhilarating and discouraging, zeroed in on the point with one question: "What do you mean when you speak of peace?"

Silence.

We didn't know what to say.

Recognizing that his young mentees were in a necessary moment of disequilibrium, our friend smiled, sat back, gestured toward the meadows, the aspen groves, and the mountains looming in the distance. "This is peace, is it not?" he asked.

On the one hand, we couldn't help but to agree. Our experience in that moment matched what we had learned about peace as a couple of young white faith leaders. We were in a beautiful place, relaxed, on a spiritual retreat, and among good friends. There was no conflict that we could see, hear, or read about on our social media feeds. All seemed "right" in the world—or at least on the porch of that particular cabin.

But on the other hand, we knew that peace meant something more than the general experience of tranquil stability or absence of conflict. We knew that the very moment of "peace" we were experiencing in the mountains was likely, at the same time, a moment of terror for countless friends around the country and world.

We knew this because we had both arrived in the mountains having just left encounters with conflict. A month earlier we were in the epicenter of the Israeli-Palestinian conflict with one of our learning delegations of US-based faith leaders. Jon had just flown to Colorado from San Diego where the immigration phenomenon was reaching a dangerous fervor. I (Jer) had just left my home in San Francisco's East Bay where the divide between the black and white communities was growing dangerously wide. While we were at ease on the porch that evening, our work had us in the thick of conflict in our neighborhoods, country, and world. We were convinced that the peace God waged in Jesus resulted in something far bigger than a sense of calm and stability for the privileged.

But to define it? We were stumped.

With the patience of a sage, our mentor listened to our silence and then watched us continue to wrestle a convincing definition of peace into existence.

At long last, once our attempts had expired, our mentor offered this counsel: "Everyone defines peace differently. The vision for peace that you have is really big and has the potential to inspire people of faith to bring it to life in ways that will change the world. But your definition needs to flow from the Scriptures. Study the Scriptures. Learn from the traditions. Let your understanding of peace pour out of the life, death, and resurrection of Jesus. And then define what it is you're hoping to bring to life in the midst of our conflicted world."

With that, the conversation concluded. But we had work to do.

SHALOM

We didn't have to look very far in the Scriptures to discover how central peace is to its story. *Shalom* is the Hebrew word translated as "peace." More than merely the absence of conflict or lack of violence, shalom indicates wholeness, completeness, fullness, salvation, and flourishing. Showing up 397 times in the Hebrew Scriptures, *shalom* is used as a greeting, a description, a desired reality, and even a name for God.

What surprised us was neither the repetition nor the various uses of the term but the fact that shalom, peace, wasn't created. Shalom is who God is. Much like we say, "God is love" or "God is hope" in our efforts to establish God as the exemplar of these qualities, we can also say, "God is peace."

With the phrase "In the beginning God . . ." (Genesis 1:1), the author is clear that before anything else existed, God was complete, fully whole, fully alive, and filled to the brim with vigor and vitality. Then, throughout the first chapter of Genesis, God is identified not through singular but plural pronouns (see Genesis 1:26). Why? Because God was and is understood as unity-in-diversity. Our triune God—later described as the Father, Son, and Spirit—lived in a constant state of mutual reciprocity, mutual submission, and diversity in function. The triune image of God is a perfect picture of community and the ultimate embodiment of peace. We can

imagine that God was totally satisfied and already wrapped up in
the experience of deepest abundance before creating anything.

Peace was real before anyone had uttered the word.

Then God, who is shalom, began to speak existence into being.
After establishing the framework of creation, God crafted the
pinnacle of his work: humanity. When the human beings woke
up, they entered a grand story and began to live their lives dancing
to the rhythm of the divine heartbeat. It was beautiful, whole, and
complete. Life as they knew it was the expanded embodiment
of peace.

We can imagine the two original human beings working together, playing together, worshiping together, imagining together,
disagreeing with each other, even making love together all in the
company of a wholly satisfied God. Humanity existed together
with God in a constant state of mutual reciprocity, mutual submission, and diversity in function.

Humanity flourished as they embraced their identity as God's
beloved, the wonder of their diversity, and the gift of being cherished by each other. Creation flourished as humanity stewarded
it with wisdom. Everything was the way it was supposed to be.
They were naked and unashamed, fully known, fully alive, fully
free (Genesis 1:27). All of existence was complete and whole. It
was peace on earth . . . for two chapters.

As suddenly as creation appeared, shalom disappeared.

It all started with a deceptive serpent (Genesis 3:1). While
seemingly innocent, the snake expressed a cunning curiosity that
began to unsettle humanity's confidence in the goodness of God.
They began to wonder whether they were truly beloved or just
pawns in a divine drama. By conversation's end, they resented the
fact that they had been created into a story of which they were
not the authors.

So, fueled by pride, they reached for the fruit of power and in so doing crossed the only boundary the Creator had established for them. Coveting authorship and longing to be in a story about themselves, they took the fruit, shared it, and ate (Genesis 3:6-7). In that moment the relationships between humanity and God, humanity and self, humanity and one another, and humanity and creation were fractured.

Conflict was born that day. Shalom—peace—was shattered. And the implications were immediate.

The couple, once fully known and cherished by the other, now chose isolation. Where nakedness had been a celebration of their belovedness by God and each other, fig-leaf garments now covered their shame. Where their words had once been of each other's beauty and virtue, now they used their voices to accuse and blame. Where once they passionately contributed to each other's flourishing, now they sought their own best interest at the other's expense. Where once they had shared a beautiful equality, now hierarchy emerged and power was wielded to subjugate. Where once the presence of God was exhilarating, now they were terrified by the nearness of the Creator.

Shalom was still God and God was still very near, but peace on earth was no more.

The garden, a place of intimacy and purpose, had been replaced with a wandering, toiling existence. Home for Adam and Eve was now a world beyond shalom. It was a world marked by uncertainty, pain, and conflict.

CONFLICT: IS IT A FOUR-LETTER WORD?

Your heart rate just quickened, didn't it? The word *conflict* slams into our bodies with the weight of painful memories. It evokes fear in some and anger in others. We all bear the scars of conflict.

For many, the word leads to memories of physical and emotional pain, relational brokenness, heartbreak, loneliness, and despair. For others, *conflict* conjures memories of guns, bombs, sexual assault, or crooked leaders. The word is associated with the loss of homes, businesses, and family members. Experiences like these have kindled a fear that causes us to avoid conflict at all costs. We learn to "keep the peace" by either absorbing the conflict or moving as far away from it as quickly as possible.

For others of us, aggression was our model. We learned at an early age that when conflict emerged, we were to win at all costs. Victory usually came through the demonstration of dominance, increased volume, and physical intimidation. So when conflict surfaces today, a familiar anger and survival instinct surges in us and we "keep the peace" by engaging the conflict armed for victory.

Our lived experiences have shaped our understanding of and behavior within conflict. But why does conflict happen?

REDEEMING CONFLICT

When God created, diversity was inevitable.

Think about it. If God is unity in diversity, then when the triune God created, the realities of diversity, distinction, and uniqueness were certain to inhabit creation. We see diversity etched into the created order: in plants and animals, the four seasons, and the unique personalities and fingerprints of humanity. Creation was and is saturated in diversity and God called it "good." Thus conflict doesn't happen because of diversity. There must be something more.

That "something more" is pride and our insatiable appetite for power, property, and status. Like those in the garden, we replace God with ourselves as author and main character of life's story, becoming the primary object of our own affection and eliminating others from our circle of concern.

Like the original two in the garden, when we grasp for the fruit of power, God becomes a threat to our fantasy and others become a threat to our survival, abundance, and status. Whenever we seek power, we prioritize ourselves over others. And every time we do this, conflict results.

Surprisingly, while it wears many faces and speaks in multiple languages, conflict is not the problem. The problems are our pride and how we choose to deal with the conflicts our pride generates.

LIFE WITHIN SHATTERED SHALOM

A conflicted world of uncertainty and pain was the setting into which two sons were born. Joy interrupted Adam and Eve's regret as Cain and then Abel entered the story. Together the four of them learned how to live within shattered shalom.

We can imagine that as Cain and Abel grew, they heard the stories of a place called "the garden." No doubt they listened to their parents talk about a far-off land and the experience of wholeness, completeness, and fullness that had saturated their lives because of their relationship with the Creator. It's as though we can hear their voices laced with regret as they recall the moment they chose rebellion, independence, and power over worshipful obedience. We can imagine them looking at their clothing and remembering out loud what it was like to be fully human, fully known, and fully cherished. We can almost see the tension in their faces as they recall the sound of shalom fracturing as they picked the fruit.

We can also imagine what it might have been like growing up in a home where the memory of peace couldn't stop the reality of conflict. It's inevitable that the two brothers watched their parents continue to seek power and experience conflict. Cain and Abel learned how to deal with conflict through their lived experience, and it resulted in bloodshed.

Cain, the elder, was a tiller of the soil, while Abel, the younger, was a cultivator of flocks. After a number of years of untold sibling rivalry, conflict came to a climax in a moment of worship. Cain brought fruit from the fields as an offering to God and Abel brought the best portions of his flocks. Cain perceived that God's favor rested on Abel's offering, and it flared in him a deep sense of competitive comparison (Genesis 4:2-5).

So Cain hatched a devious plan that resulted in the violent, bloody death of his little brother (Genesis 4:8). As Abel's blood soaked into the soil, God entered the story with an important, life-defining question for Cain: "Where is your little brother?"

"I don't know," replied Cain. "Am I my brother's keeper?" (Genesis 4:9).

While God's question sought to bring Cain into a visceral understanding of what he had just done, Cain's question was a declaration.

"I am not linked to nor responsible for the shalom of my brother."

Grasping for the fruit of power had led Cain to disregard the humanity, dignity, and image of God in his own kin. Cain abandoned his vocation to be his brother's keeper and shalom continued to shatter.

THE JOURNEY TOWARD SHALOM

Just a few generations later, God launched a scandalous and costly peacemaking campaign. It all started with a barren couple named Abram and Sarai. God invited these two to leave the comfort of their home and to start a family in a new land. The lure was a divine three-part promise: God would multiply their family into a great nation, God would give them a physical location on the globe, and God would utilize them as a physical presence of blessing to all the nations. Through their family, peace would be restored in the world (Genesis 12:1-3).

Because they were old and had no children, Abram and Sarai, renamed Abraham and Sarah, were unsure of the viability of God's promise. So God made an unbreakable, sealed-in-blood promise to them.

In accordance with the customs of the day, Abraham was instructed by God to split five animals in two, creating a blood-filled pathway. Each party was to walk the blood path and in so doing commit to a covenant with one another. Both understood that their own blood would be spilled if they failed to keep their commitment (Genesis 15:7-10; see also Jeremiah 11).

However, once Abraham had prepared the blood path, God did a startling thing. Abraham fell into a deep, terrifying sleep, and God appeared as a smoking firepot and burning torch, walking the blood path twice (Genesis 15:12-21). In so doing God signed the blood covenant unilaterally—essentially signing it for himself *and* for Abraham. This was God's declaration that if he didn't hold up his end of the bargain, he would die. It was also God's declaration that if Abraham's family couldn't remain faithful to God, *God would die.* God was confident in his ability to live up to the agreement, and he put his own blood on the line on behalf of Abraham and his descendants.

This covenant exposed God's commitment to restoration: it would come at the cost of spilled blood. Rather than that of an animal, the blood that would restore peace to earth would be God's.

As the Genesis narrative continues, we discover that God's plan for peace goes against the human impulse for power. We pick up with a conflict that erupted between two women. With the promise of an expansive family echoing in her heart, Sarah, still barren, took matters into her own hands. She presented her servant Hagar to Abraham, and together they conceived (Genesis 16:1-4).

Even though this had all been Sarah's idea, no doubt the thought of someone else's little boy in her tents sparked her competitiveness and caused her to question her role in the promise. With her status threatened and her pride wounded, and with the pain of her infertility searing and her Egyptian servant gloating, a dangerous conflict came to a head. Sarah's jealousy accelerated and she reached for the fruit of power.

She couldn't bring herself to kill like Cain, so Sarah mistreated Hagar until she fled. Exile was pregnant Hagar's death sentence (Genesis 16:6). Similar to Cain, Sarah's need for power and status caused her to disregard her responsibility for her sister's shalom.

Thankfully, this particular episode didn't result in blood-soaked soil. God searched for Hagar, found her, restored her dignity, and blessed her future. Hagar survived the conflict, but we're left to wonder if the fractured relationship between Sarah and Hagar was ever restored.

Years later, just as God had promised, Sarah conceived and gave birth to a son (Genesis 21:1-5). She named him Isaac, and God promised Isaac a future of countless offspring. Over time that promise came true as Isaac married Rebekah, who gave birth to a set of twins. Another pair of brothers began a journey through conflict and toward shalom (Genesis 25:19-26).

From conception these brothers were destined to live in conflict with each other. The eldest, Esau, was a wild outdoorsman and the youngest, Jacob, a cunning deceiver. Jacob was strategic and driven by his pursuit of status. Esau was impulsive and fueled by his appetite (Genesis 25:27-34).

Their relationship was a toxic cocktail that ended up costing Esau both his birthright and his father's blessing (Genesis 27:36). Jacob's pursuit of personal gain was successful. Esau hated him for it and so began to plot his brother's demise. In this case both parties reached for the fruit of power, and another death sentence would have been enacted had Jacob not run away. The conflict that had simmered for years caused two brothers to reject each other. The thin threads of relationship were severed and physical distance between them left little hope that shalom would be restored.

Years went by before we find Jacob on his way back toward Esau (Genesis 32:1-5). As Jacob's family drew near, Esau began his own journey toward Jacob. When they saw each other, Jacob braced for a death blow, but Esau offered a kiss (Genesis 33:1-4). The circle of violence had finally been broken and shalom had been restored.

But not for long.

In the final deadly conflict in the Genesis narrative, Jacob, renamed Israel, lavished his favoritism on the oldest son of his most cherished wife. Joseph was his name and, like his father, he lacked tact when it came to family relationships.

He shared his dreams featuring his own rise to power freely with his older brothers (Genesis 37:3-11). These dreams, combined with the experience of being demoted by the young dreamer, caused the brothers' jealousy to grow. Their egos were wounded and they hated Joseph. The only shalom they cared to envision was one in which Joseph was no more.

Before they knew it, the opportunity presented itself. Israel had sent Joseph on a mission to seek the shalom of his brothers (Genesis 37:12-14). When at last Joseph found them, they were so intoxicated by jealousy that they threw him into an empty cistern (Genesis 37:22-24). Joseph's crimes of favoritism and arrogance merited a sentence of death by exposure.

Ironically, it was Joseph's brothers' greed that intervened: they rescued the dreamer from death and sold him as a slave (Genesis 37:28).

Years went by in which Joseph transitioned from a slave in a foreign land to an unjustly incarcerated criminal and, ultimately, to the second-most-powerful administrator in the Egyptian empire. It was from this place of power that Joseph sought the shalom not only of Egypt but of the entire region. Israel's offspring was causing the shalom of the nations.

Meanwhile, sheer desperation for survival brought the brothers to their knees before Joseph without knowing who he was. Their humility produced a compassion in Joseph that resulted in merciful action. He reconciled with his brothers. As the fractured relationships were restored, the entire family flourished.

From the conclusion of Genesis forward, the biblical story is saturated with the faithfulness and presence of a peacemaking God and the wandering elusiveness of a power-hungry people. Throughout the remainder of the Old Testament God made himself known to a particular bloodline for the sake of all bloodlines. God guided his people through unthinkable odds into liberation and never stopped reminding them whose they were, who they were, and why they were on the planet. God made his physical dwelling among them and repeatedly invited them into the adventure of faithfulness.

Despite his people's fickle temperament and appetite-driven worship, God offered them a way to be right with him, with themselves, and with one another. Over and again God invited Abraham's family to participate in making peace real in the world, but they never embraced their peacemaking vocation. God was going to have to do something more powerful and potent than ever to bring about the holistic repair of severed relationships.

EMBRACING AN ELUSIVE DEFINITION

And there it is. After a careful study of Genesis and beyond, we find the definition of peace that has been eluding us. Rather than the absence of conflict and presence of justice, peace is the abundance of wholeness, completeness, and fullness that emerges on the other side of holistically repaired, formerly severed relationships. Peace is what the world will look like when individuals embrace their identity as God's beloved and their vocation as seekers of their sister's and brother's shalom. Peace is what the world will look like when broken relationships are no longer broken, when unjust systems are renovated or replaced for the flourishing of all. Peace is what the world will look like when we understand diversity not as a problem to solve but as a beautiful reality to embrace such that we all become more fully alive.

When we speak of peace, we can call to mind the ancient Japanese pottery tradition called *Kintsugi*. With this technique, a clay vessel is broken and then put back together, but not in its original form. Instead the restoration process involves the use of pure gold to mend the divides and heal the fissures. The broken vessel is put back together in such a way that it is stronger and more beautiful than before it was broken. In Kintsugi, the scars tell beautiful stories of healing and restoration rather than painful stories of destruction.

Peace is the holistic repair of severed relationships. When it is realized, our relationships are stronger and more beautiful than before they were broken.

Understood this way, peace is not waged when, after a relationship has been severed, two parties apologize, compromise, and then treat one another with polite indifference. Peace is not waged when an unjust system and power differential is allowed to remain in place for the benefit of a few. Peace is not waged when distrust and resentment are given space to fester and grow.

Peace is only realized when justice is accompanied by the experience of forgiveness, mercy, healing, and compassion. Peace is waged when, after a relationship has been fractured and repaired, we who were once enemies choose to stand together as friends, allies, advocates, even family, committed to co-creating a more beautiful, just, mutually beneficial future.

Now, lest we imagine this kind of peace as a human-initiated and human-accomplished endeavor, let's return one final time to the garden. As our journey continues, we'll discover that our pursuit of peace is simply the embodiment of the peacemaking priority and practice of God.

REFLECT AND DISCUSS

1. How would you define peace? Is the peace you speak of attainable and, if so, how do you see your role in ushering it in?

2. What has experience taught you about conflict? What are the habits you live out in the midst of conflict and what have they cost you?

3. Consider again the conflict you identified at the end of the last chapter. What were your contributions to the fractured relationship? What are your contributions to maintaining the divide? What have been your attempts at restoration?

THREE

THE DIVINE PATTERN

We remember when our picture of God had nothing to do with peace. From early on we were taught that Joshua fought the battle of Jericho (there's a song in your head now, isn't there?) and that God was enthusiastically behind it. In fact, as the stories go, the annihilation of cities inhabited by men, women, children, and newborn babies was the stuff of righteous obedience for Joshua and the tribes of Israel.

But if we considered what happened to Jericho in a contemporary light, we would call it genocide—a term that conjures up images from Armenia, Jewish Europe, Cambodia, Rwanda, Bosnia, Darfur, Syria, and a tragic number of others. As we consider those atrocities, we have to ask, is God an endorsing warlord or an everyday peacemaker?

Our early discipleship constructed an image of a God who was strong, violent at times, white, and male, with little regard for foreign bloodlines. Over time this image became calcified in our understanding of who God is, who God is for, and who God is indifferent toward. For a couple of white male Christians, this image of God was convenient in that it kept God in our image. It invited us to remain at ease in the seat of power and helped us justify our indifference to, exclusion of, and violence against those who were not like "us." For if God, who looks like "us," ordered the elimination of foreign bloodlines, then wasn't it okay for us to exclude them from our communities or to celebrate their demise?

In our own personal journeys and through our work, we've come to lament that our picture of God has been more informed by the bloodied walls of Jericho than by the blood-stained cross of Christ. The former is an image of God that, far from portraying peacemaking, reinforces power and the use of violence against others to secure victory. It's an ethnocentric construction that disregards the dark tone of God's human flesh and the fact that the blood of the nations coursed through God's veins. The genocidal warrior image ignores the great surprise that when God entered creation, he did so not enthroned as king but as a child born into the impoverished underside of the Roman Empire.

We've had to work out the incongruence of the Sunday school portrayal of God with what we discover in Jesus and what we understand occurred on the cross. If Jesus is the image of God (John 14:6-14), then when God became most visible to humanity and demonstrated the most power, he looked not like a warlord but like a slaughtered lamb. That selfless sacrifice brought about the restoration that changed everything for all of humanity and all of creation. The cross of Christ exposes God not as a white, powerful, violent warrior, but as an others-oriented, nations-embracing, enemy-loving peacemaker.

Imagine our surprise when this new, more accurate, Jesus-informed construction of a peacemaking God emerged. Then imagine our shock when we realized that God's commitment to peacemaking didn't begin with Jesus but culminated with him. That's right. From the moment humanity picked the fruit, God had been wholeheartedly committed to the restoration of all things. God's pattern of peacemaking had its roots in the garden.

THE ROOTS OF EVERYDAY PEACEMAKING

In the wake of the fruit picking, God saw the shattered state of creation. God saw both the shards of peace and his image in those he cherished. God saw their humanity and their dignity. God saw their inability to find their way back into restored relationships with him, themselves, each other, and creation. God saw their potential and the opportunity conflict had provided for their relationship to deepen. God saw it all, and what God saw became the most important thing in the world to him.

Rather than walking away, God immersed into creation. God immersed into the radical center of a conflicted story in pursuit of those who were no longer at peace with him, themselves, each other, or creation. When God immersed, he did so not with weapons to destroy but with tools to transform. With compassion and mercy, our peacemaking God pursued restoration rather than destruction (Genesis 3:8-9).

When at last God found humanity after they had picked the fruit, they were isolated from one another and sewing fig leaves together in an effort to further insolate themselves from intimacy (Genesis 3:7). Where peace was once expressed in full disclosure, life in conflict meant they no longer wanted to be closely known by God or each other. It was then and there that God contended for them in a costly and creative way.

God's contending that day set the bar for how he would contend for humanity's restoration from that moment forward: the cost was spilled blood (Genesis 3:8-21). Because of humanity's

reach for power, death entered the story. It was not the blood of
those who rebelled that was spilled; instead God took the life
of animals in order to tailor clothing that would cover the
shame of those who bore his image.

From that moment forward, the trajectory toward restoration
was guided by a peacemaking God who would continue to see,
immerse, and contend. Starting in Egypt, God taught Israel how
to follow him and in so doing contribute to the restoration of the
whole world. They were to be the image-bearers of God: global
peacemakers who ushered in God's world by seeing the image of
God in others, immersing themselves into their stories, and contending for their flourishing. Unfortunately, they kept reaching
for the fruit of power instead of the companionship of God and
the hands of their foreign neighbors.

God's response? He repeatedly made himself known to them,
dwelled among them, demonstrated faithfulness, advocated for
them, and offered a way for them to be made right with God,
each other, their neighbors, and all of creation. But rather than
taking advantage of the power and presence of their peacemaking God, the people continued to reject their identity and
vocation. Like the original couple, they experienced fractured
relationships and continued to journey from the land of promise
farther into exile.

It was from within Babylon that the people cried out to God
to make good on his promises to Abraham. They longed for God
to decisively restore the peace that was shattered in the garden.
As they cried out, the voices of the faithful rose up. Through the
prophets, God reassured the family that he saw the plight of his
exiled people and would again immerse into the radical center of
it. Just like in the garden, God promised to contend for their
flourishing and restore all the severed relationships at the cost of
his own blood.

Then God was silent for four hundred years. Finally, he spoke to an impoverished couple in Galilee, saying to them, "The time has come. I'm making good on my promise" (Matthew 1:18-25; Luke 1:5–2:45).

God had continued to see his image in humanity. God had continued to see their pain and their plight. However, rather than immersing himself into the center of it with the fanfare of a hero, God immersed into their brokenness encased in the flesh of a fully dependent human baby. God was human. Therefore God could bleed.

In the short years of Jesus' life, God unceasingly demonstrated his ability to see humanity. Jesus consistently contended for both the marginalized and the powerful by humbly immersing himself into their broken lives with wisdom, compassion, and healing. Again and again we watch Jesus restore the health, identity, and dignity of the sick, oppressed, possessed, impoverished, uncertain, deceived, and accused.

Beyond that, Jesus was adamantly opposed to any and every system, structure, political entity, empire, and kingdom that did not reflect the just, compassionate, restorative reign of God. While Jesus' contending was at times healing, there were also moments when it resembled activism. Not only was Jesus critical of the religious and political systems of his day, he contended for all involved by directly speaking truth to power and standing in the way of injustice. This is the kind of contending that ultimately cost Jesus his life.

In the teachings of Jesus, God demonstrated that he could see the pain and plight of the people. Jesus contended for the souls and bodies of both the sick and the healthy as well as for the restoration of broken systems that broke down human lives. In his Sermon on the Mount, Jesus blessed those who would follow in his restorative steps as peacemakers, calling them "children of

God" (Matthew 5:9). Jesus spent the remainder of that and future teachings connecting human relationships to human flourishing and revealing a God who would stop at nothing to see creation reconciled to its Creator.

Ultimately, it was on the cross that God demonstrated just how much he saw and cherished us. Immersed in the most severe of human torture, Jesus contended, at the cost of his blood, for the restoration of relationship between humanity and God. In Jesus' resurrection, God restored shalom between us and God, us and ourselves, us and one another, and us and creation (Colossians 1:19-20).

The restoration of all things was in God's view from the very beginning. God is the great peacemaker who established the priority of peace and the practice of peacemaking throughout history. God, in Jesus, embodied the peacemaking practices of *see*, *immerse*, and *contend* in order to restore shalom. In the life and death of Jesus, God waged the decisive peace promised to Abraham. The resurrection confirmed that all things were reconciled to God. And as Paul revealed in his second letter to the Corinthians, God intends for this established peace to be made real in the world through followers of Jesus (2 Corinthians 5:18-20).

Peacemaking is the mission of God and the vocation of God's people. While it's hard work, peacemaking is neither a strategy to employ nor an obligation to uphold. It is a life fueled by our identity as the reconciled beloved.

EMBRACING OUR IDENTITY AS THE RECONCILED BELOVED

I (Jer) grew up in the Midwest in the home of courageous Jesus-following parents. I knew the stories of Moses and the exodus, Joshua's Jericho conquest, and Jonah's whale. I was compelled by the stories of Jesus' miracles and inspired by that original community of followers. I understood that Jesus was God on the earth and that when Jesus showed up, things changed for people. I recognized the pressure to follow Jesus and to do my part to ensure that other people followed Jesus too. But I'm not sure I understood why. Cognitively, I was impressed by Jesus, but my confusion about the why of following him diminished my desire to live into the adventure.

Then, when I was nineteen, everything changed.

As a nominal, cultural Christian, I applied to work as a counselor at a Bible camp among the northern lakes of Wisconsin. I had the ability to write in a way that made my testimony sparkle on the application and possessed enough charisma to charm my way through the interview. But it wasn't until I was offered a spot on the counseling team that I realized just how over my head I was.

We spent the first week, training week, in the Scriptures, learning the big story of God from start to finish. It was the first time I recognized that our story, which began in a garden and will finish in a new city, was fully inhabited and animated by an invested, collaborative God. As I narrated that story over and over again for ten weeks, it began to work itself into my DNA. The story was unlocked from the flannel graphs of my imagination and I began to consider the implications of living the God life. Over those weeks Jesus shifted from an otherworldly miracle worker to the embodiment of a God who couldn't hold himself back from fixing what we had broken in the garden.

On the last day of camp I found myself across a picnic table from an eighteen-year-old camper. The gentle rain that fell that afternoon wrinkled the pages of our Bibles, but either we didn't notice or we didn't care. We were completely consumed by a conversation about a God who had put on flesh and come into our neighborhood and died so that we could be redeemed, reconciled, and restored.

Near the conversation's end, my camper, who was really more of a peer, leaned back and whispered, "I'm worth God's Son." Shaking his head in bewilderment, he repeated that phrase over and over.

"I'm worth God's Son. I'm worth God's Son. I'm worth God's Son!"

Jonas had never said "Yes!" to Jesus before, and I'm not entirely sure I had either. In hindsight, it's clear that God was in the process of restoring the fractured relationships between himself and us.

Jonas went on to declare his "Yes!" to Jesus that afternoon. As I listened to him pray and watched him run to the cabin to share the news with his friends, something significant dawned on me: the Spirit of God that I had been talking about all summer had just worked to transform Jonas into the reconciled beloved.

Two weeks later, with Jonas's phrase, *I'm worth God's Son!* echoing in my mind, I too joined the ranks of the reconciled beloved. I was compelled by the life of Jesus, but what undid me was gaining a sense of what God thought about me.

Your identity and mine, according to God, is the reconciled beloved. Let that sink in! We are reconciled to a God of extravagant love who loves us because he wants to. If that's true, then we no longer have to live hindered by image management and legalism. Embracing our identity as the reconciled beloved unshackles us to imitate the one who loves us so.

In his letter to the church in Ephesus, Paul called the Jesus community to "follow God's example, therefore, as dearly loved children and walk in the way of love, just as Christ loved us and gave himself up for us as a fragrant offering and sacrifice to God" (Ephesians 5:1-2). There are two words for "children" that Paul chose from to express the experience of being God's child. The first, *huios*, is used to describe the general experience of a being a son or daughter. The word carries with it a very generic kind of love that God would have for the entire world.

The second word, and the one Paul selected here, is *tekna*. This word reflects an only child's experience of receiving all the love from both of her parents. It's the quality of love that results in a child being fully secure in her identity as the beloved. It is here that we encounter the unspeakable quality of God's love: God is able to love us as though each of us were his only child. God loves each of us with the kind of love that does whatever needs to be done for our relationship to be fully restored.

What is the appropriate response to that kind of love? Imitation. We want to be just like the one who loves us extravagantly and who did whatever it took to mend the divide between us. It is out of our identity as the reconciled and our experience of being God's beloved that our lives begin to reflect the costly, creative, restorative activity of God.

We imitate a peacemaking God because we are his beloved kids. Our imitation begins with one another.

RECONCILED TO ONE ANOTHER

Throughout Jesus' life and teachings, he continually invited his disciples to understand their identity not only as autonomous individuals, but as a living, breathing, interdependent community that was to embody and bear witness to the good news of God's kingdom. Central to their communal identity was their ability to live reconciled to one another (Matthew 5:22-24). They didn't have the option to internalize their resentment and carry it with them. Unresolved conflict and resentment would have contaminated the community. Neither did they have the option to move toward conflict in unhelpful ways that only widened the divides. They had to commit to a regular practice of confession, repentance, forgiveness, and understanding (Matthew 18).

This was important not only for the sake of maintaining the community's integrity and common mission; it was important because how the community lived with and loved one another was a direct reflection of the one they followed. John's Gospel gives an account of Jesus praying to God for unity among his followers because he understood the sacramental power of oneness. In those lonely moments, Jesus prayed for their unity because he understood that the watching world would discover the truth about who God is and experience his tangible love for them by watching the Jesus community live in reconciled oneness (John 17:20-24).

If the neighbors of these early Jesus-followers saw only a community in relational disarray, what would that say of Jesus? What would their disunity communicate about the stability of the peace Jesus had accomplished on the cross?

Recently we found ourselves around a table with a team of faith leaders from an influential Midwestern church. Their restlessness was palpable.

"Peace has been one of our core values for years," they said, "but our community is saturated with conflict. It's pervasive! Will you help us?"

When we asked them to describe the implications of their dilemma, they spoke of a conflict-saturated staff culture, the inability to experience healthy disagreement among leaders and volunteers, the uptick of marriages and families within the church dissolving, and an inability to collaborate with other local churches to address local issues. The leaders went on to express their sense of helplessness as they watched issues of racism and injustice surge in their neighborhoods and armed conflicts accelerate around the world. They were immersed in an insurmountable sea of conflict and they had no idea how to swim.

At last, they disclosed just how far their church was from the reality of peace: "We're experts at identifying, discussing, and gossiping about conflict, but ultimately, we choose to either ignore it, run away from it, or engage it violently." As we dug in with this team, we asked them to consider how they were contributing to the conflicts in the church. It was a risky question to ask a bunch of leaders who had spent more time diagnosing the problem then examining their own motives, intentions, and behavior. Not surprisingly, they were up for considering the possibility that they had helped seed and perpetuate conflict. By meal's end, they had begun the hard work of acknowledging how their pride and pursuit of power had created a culture of conflict in the congregation. They realized that if they wanted to become an embodiment of peace in their city, they first needed to confront their own pride, repent of it, and begin moving through rather than around the conflicts that existed within the family.

It's troubling how many times we have worked with those of other faiths and traditions whose view of the church is one of infighting, hatred, and division. It's time to recognize that our words of "peace" mean nothing if they emerge from the simmering ashes of broken relationships, turf wars, and theological witch hunts. In our view, the church has not only abdicated its vocation to be an instrument of peace; we haven't even been a neutral presence in our cities. Instead, our divisiveness, interfamily competition, and unresolved conflict have been detracting from the movement and witness of peace God made real in Jesus. If the church is going to be an instrument of peace in the world, we have got to lead by example in our own communities.

We were recently with a collection of pastors in San Diego and were asked to share about our common call to peacemaking. Fully aware of the posturing and isolation of many of these churches, we found it a sacred experience to see these individuals gathered together representing their respective communities. Also fully aware of the inherent tension resting under the surface, we opened with this: "If the apostle Paul were still around and wrote a letter to the church in San Diego, it wouldn't be labeled First Presbyterian, First Baptist, Calvary, Evangelical Covenant, or any other denominational name. It would be labeled 'the Church of San Diego.'"

It was as profound and convicting as it was simple. Of course! We are one community submitted to the rule and reign of Jesus in this city, but we find far too many ways to insulate, isolate, and divide. We closed with the implications of our ability to live a reconciled presence: "We have been called to be a living sign of the peace that was waged in Jesus and to join God in healing a broken world. If we can't learn to live together, collaborate, encourage, and endorse one another, we are not a sign of peace but of anti-peace, anti-kingdom, and anti-Jesus."

As everyday peacemakers who have been reconciled to God, we must be reconciled ourselves. Our lives must demonstrate dependence on God and one another. It's here that we will find our strength, identity, and fuel to live as those united for God's mission of restoration.

THE PROBLEM OF DIS-INTEGRATION

While peace is central to the heart and activity of God, the prevalence of conflict indicates that peacemaking has been dis-integrated from our understanding of who God is, what God did in Jesus, what God is doing now, and what role we get to play in it.

How is it that we've dismissed peacemaking as unrealistic or discarded it altogether? Perhaps a brief exploration of history will shift confusion to understanding and help us reintegrate peacemaking as our central practice as followers of Jesus.

If we were to rewind the clock to the turn of the twentieth century, we'd discover the emergence of a theological framework

known as "dispensationalism." Developed in England and made
popular in the United States by John Nelson Darby and the Scofield Notes Bible, this theology suggests that God has chosen to
deal differently with humanity in different eras, or dispensations.
Darby suggested that we are currently in the sixth of seven dispensations—the age of grace (see Romans 5:20-21; Ephesians 3:1-9)—and that this current era will conclude with the
resurrection of dead believers and the rapture of living followers
of Jesus. This rapture, an exit-hatch strategy central to dispensationalism (see 1 Thessalonians 4:17), will supposedly initiate a
seven-year tribulation that will conclude with the second coming
of Jesus and the battle of Armageddon. It is believed that Jesus'
victory in this battle will usher in the seventh dispensation, a
thousand-year reign of God called the millennial kingdom (see
Isaiah 9:6-7; 11:1-9; Revelation 20:1-6).

Having made its way into most evangelical seminaries,
Scofield's extrabiblical commentary has led generations of pastors
to embrace this relatively recent theological framework as a nor-
mative reading of Scripture. It is a reading that identifies God's
declared plan in the world as moving everything toward a violent
end—an atomic holocaust that will usher in the second return of
Christ. Such a theology renders peacemaking as not only a waste
of time, but also antithetical to what God is doing in the world.
Dispensationalism generates a form of faithfulness that looks
more like survival than participation and requires us to label and
avoid our enemies rather than know and love them. This
framework removes humanity from playing a redemptive role in
the very story God commissioned us to and encourages us to
endorse war and violence, especially in the Middle East, as both
move us closer to Christ's return. It disregards the cross as the
decisive victory and the formal inauguration of the kingdom of
God on earth as it is in heaven.

Accompanying the emergence of dispensationalism were two devastating world wars and the carnage of atomic bombs. Soon after we found ourselves in another active military campaign in Vietnam and in the midst of the civil rights movement. A faux "peace" being waged through military strength and political power wove dispensational theology deeper into our evangelical framework. Proponents and tenets of peacemaking and non-violent resistance were seen as fringe, soft, euphoric, and idealistic. Bombs kept the peace, not human beings.

And then, at the turn of the twenty-first century, terror crashed into our national symbols of strength and security, causing our country to experience the pain of loss and the fear of an unknown future. We were left with a critical decision of how we would respond: revenge or reconciliation?

After 9/11 we discovered just how far peacemaking had been separated from our understanding of God, our mission, and our vocation. Still reeling from an unthinkable attack, the United States had an opportunity to be the foremost instrument of peace in the world and its church had the opportunity to lead the way. However, in a moment when ninety percent of Americans polled said they had turned to prayer and religion to cope with the pain and stress, our national desire for revenge trumped our Christian imperative for reconciliation. A war on terror was launched and the face of our enemies became Arab Muslims.

Now conflict and painful division seem to saturate our world. International elections have resulted in the demonization of already marginalized and vulnerable populations. Contemporary armed conflicts have claimed millions of lives and have displaced millions of others. Racialized violence is accelerating in the streets of our country. Neighbors and family members continue reaching for the fruit of power rather than one another's hands, resulting in painful schisms.

If in the life, death, and resurrection of Jesus God waged a decisive peace, why do we still live in a world plagued by such conflict? Why do hostile divisions dominate the planet? Why do ethnic strife, racial animosity, gross economic inequality, and international conflict destroy the lives of countless millions? Why, within the reality of the peace waged through the blood of Jesus, are

- our brothers and sisters still killing each other?
- our women and children still being sold for the sexual pleasure of men?
- our men, women, and children still being owned and used by greedy power brokers?
- our streets still flooding with the tears of mothers who have lost their children to senseless gun violence?
- our immigrants still hiding, hopelessly, in fear, in the shadows of overcrowded apartments?
- our refugees still holding desperately to the keys of their homes and the hope of their right to return?
- our indigenous tribes still finding themselves sequestered to the corners and restricted within fences?
- addictions to chemicals, images, and violence still robbing the future of untold millions?
- our people still going hungry while enough food to feed the world over is thrown away?
- our poor still building dwellings they will never live in and planting and harvesting fields that they will never own?
- our children still dying from curable ailments?
- our little boys and girls without parents still finding themselves trapped in a saturated foster care system without safe places and people to call home?

Why?

Because the peace God waged in Jesus becomes tangible only as we embrace our identity as the reconciled beloved, God's mission as peacemaking, and our vocation as everyday peacemakers. This is the adventure we have been saved into.

REFLECT AND DISCUSS

1. When you imagine God, what is the picture that immediately comes to mind? What are the primary elements (teachers, Bible studies, relationships, experiences) that have shaped that picture?

2. What obstacles or experiences of betrayal make it challenging for us to embrace our identity as the reconciled beloved? How would your life be different if you lived like you believed that you are the reconciled beloved?

3. If the Christian community is a sign to the world that reflects who God is, what does the watching world learn about God by watching your family live? Your church? The church in your region?

4. How has dispensationalism informed your understanding of God and mission? Yourself and those different from you? The end times? How has dispensationalism impacted your participation in God's mission?

FOUR

EVERYDAY CONFLICT, EVERYDAY PEACEMAKING

At seventeen years old, I (Jon) remember preparing a speech for my high school English class, thinking, "This is finally my chance to expose my classmates and teacher for how wrong they are and how right I am. If I can just offer enough statistics and well-constructed arguments, I can prove to them that my Christian worldview is superior to their godless worldview."

I proceeded to present an articulate—and angry—case for how my understanding of Christianity had been silenced and how it should be integrated into all areas of social and political engagement.

Ironically, at seventeen I "knew all the answers" to the same questions I now wrestle with. Further, without diminishing who I was and the journey I was on, I am embarrassed by the hostile, combative, and judgmental posture in which I articulated my "answers."

I grew up in a Jesus-loving home with a family that was relentless in its pursuit of living out our core convictions. I am deeply grateful for the foundation I was given as a result. That said, my understanding of discipleship was at best incomplete and, at worst, completely contrary to the one I claimed to follow. As I matured in my life and faith through trusted mentors, global engagement, and my study of Jesus and the Gospels, I began to question my inherited understanding of faithful discipleship. I began to stumble toward a Jesus who taught and lived an others-oriented way of life as the embodiment of an enemy-loving God.

As I took an honest inventory, I began to confront the fact that while I had believed and said the "right" things, my life was becoming more and more isolated from the very people, places, and realities Jesus gave his primary attention to. He introduced the world to a kingdom where the first would be last and the last would be first, yet my relationships largely reflected the inverse.

My discipleship journey led me to believe that "the other" was a threat to my faith. Jesus said it was in the eyes of "the other" that we would see God (Matthew 25:35-40).

My discipleship journey led me to believe that "the enemy" was to be destroyed. Jesus said "the enemy" was to be loved and prayed for (Matthew 5:43-44).

My discipleship journey condoned the use of violence to kill "the enemy" when necessary. On behalf of restoring "the enemy," Jesus was a willing recipient of violence at the cost of his own life.

While each believer has been on his or her own unique faith journey, my experience as part of the evangelical church in America tells me that many of you probably can relate to this fragmented and disembodied form of discipleship in one way or another.

How had my understanding and practice of discipleship become so counter to the life and teachings of a dark-skinned, first-century Jewish rabbi living under Roman occupation in Palestine? How had I missed out on understanding peacemaking as the mission of God and the vocation of God's people?

First, I had inherited an understanding of discipleship that shaped my identity around right belief and practice rather than understanding my identity as the reconciled beloved. In this pseudo form of discipleship, morality was prioritized over spirituality. Morality is about saying and doing the "right" things. Spirituality is the process of becoming fully human by allowing the Spirit to form and inform my everyday participation with God in healing a broken world.

Where morality can make us slaves of "do's and don'ts" as a means to achieve our belovedness, spirituality is a living, breathing invitation to embrace who we were created to be all along. Morality is often helpful in identifying what we are against, but spirituality calls us to identify and champion what we are for.

How often do we hear Christian leaders using their platforms to condemn and point fingers rather than remind us of our identity as the reconciled beloved and send us into our wild, refreshing, hope-filled vocation as everyday peacemakers?

Second, my understanding of faithfulness was defined by words like *defense*, *safety*, *security*, and *morality*. While none of these are inherently bad or wrong, they certainly don't reflect a holistic picture of faithfulness as we witness in the life and teachings of Jesus.

When played out in real life, these words lead to an entrenched faith that seeks to escape our world rather than a faith rooted in deep conviction—a faith that intentionally moves toward conflict, difference, and disagreement equipped to heal rather than to win. Jesus lived his life alongside all the "wrong" people who should have been a threat to his religion and way of life. He invites us into a renewed understanding of faithfulness as a movement toward and alongside "the other" rather than a posture of defense that leads to isolation and insulation.

In Matthew's Gospel, Jesus confronts the religious elite who were doing all the "right" things, like tithing ten percent, learning Torah, and offering sacrifices: "Woe to you, teachers of the law and Pharisees, you hypocrites! You give a tenth of your spices— mint, dill and cumin. But you have neglected the more important matters of the law—justice, mercy and faithfulness. You should have practiced the latter, without neglecting the former" (Matthew 23:23).

The religious elite weren't trying to miss the point, but their understanding of discipleship had turned into a contest over who could become the most pious and "faithful" in ways that simply didn't matter if they weren't leading to justice and mercy. For them, faithfulness took the form of personal isolation and insulation. For Jesus, faithfulness took the form of selfless service, sacrifice, and radical presence in the mud and muck of everyday life.

In the end I have had to come to terms with the fact that the discipleship of my youth was at the very least incomplete. At the same time I have been awakened to a renewed under- standing of discipleship that has connected me strongly to my identity as the reconciled beloved. I'm alive to the ways God is inviting me to step off the hamster wheel of morality and into a life-giving spirituality, liberating me into the fullness of God's mission of peacemaking.

Our American evangelical Christian constructs have often held us captive to a discipleship paradigm that is more focused on climbing a ladder of intellectual morality than catalyzing us into a cross-shaped life that reflects the Jesus we talk about.

Well over a decade after giving that speech in my high school English class, I returned to the campus and the same teacher who had endured my verbal onslaught. This time I didn't enter to condemn and judge; I came to apologize. I thanked these individuals for their grace, understanding, and contribution to my journey of following Jesus in a way that looked more like love than condemnation.

The discipleship journey that led to this apology was (and continues to be) unexpected, disorienting, and extremely necessary. It is to that journey we now turn.

PEACEMAKING AS DISCIPLESHIP

One of our mentors in the ways of peace is Lynne Hybels. She's the cofounder of Willow Creek Community Church in Chicago who, in countless ways among numerous people, embodies the practices of everyday peacemaking. Lynne courageously, humbly, and strategically invites others into this movement. As she reflected on peacemaking, Lynne pointed out that this is a costly way of life. Rather than the next fad for the North American church to embrace, peacemaking needs to be "the next frontier of discipleship." That is, following Jesus is both a classroom and an adventure that forms us, equips us, and activates us into a life of everyday peacemaking.

If this is true, peacemakers are not born and peacemaking is not something we add on to our experience of following Jesus. Instead, everyday peacemakers are formed and peacemaking is the expression of our lives as we follow the crucified and resurrected one. In following Jesus our trajectory is reoriented toward others and our priority becomes the flourishing of all. As we follow the Jesus we so eloquently speak of, we find ourselves joining God in ushering in a new world.

If following Jesus is the formational journey, then our definitions and experiences of discipleship must expand. They need to carry us far beyond the sterile intellectual classrooms that teach us to master content and be nice to one another. To become everyday peacemakers, we must find ourselves mastered by the author of the content and learn to follow the promptings of the Spirit toward what is broken in our world. As we do so, seeing, immersing, and contending will become the practices of our lives and restoration will spring to life all around us.

This is the same formational journey that Jesus invited his disciples—the first everyday peacemakers—into. If you recall, he invited them not into the classroom but into the beauty, pain, joy, and injustice of life under Roman occupation. He desired not that his followers would be smarter, nicer, and more socially adapted than anyone else. Rather, his chief aim was to restore a broken world, and his strategy was to teach those aspiring peacemakers to live in and love a broken world with him.

It was a costly journey that Jesus invited those disciples into. The parts of them that didn't look like Jesus were identified, tilled up, and transformed. It was also a riveting journey in that they got to join Jesus in making wrong things right in the world. And it was a comprehensive journey. Yes, it involved teaching, but it also included bizarre invitations, uncommon friendships, and the subversion of any system that opposed the kingdom of God. While Jesus trained his followers in contemplative reflection, he also pushed them into experiments they weren't prepared for where they experienced both success and failure. Ultimately, he took them to the cross where he taught them that peace is ushered in not through military overthrow but selfless sacrifice.

DAILY REALITY OF CONFLICT

Conflict is all around us every day. Five minutes on Facebook reveals our growing inability to engage with others: opinions fly, tempers boil, and feelings morph into hostile dehumanization. This is true online, in our homes, in our workplaces and communities, and on the other side of the world.

Conflict, hatred, and injustice are becoming the norm. Both close to home and around the globe, broken systems break people. In our communities, neighborhoods are disintegrating based on race, orientation, documentation, and association. On an interpersonal level, we are unable to engage in constructive discourse, exchanging it for debate and posturing.

Peacemaking isn't a reaction to conflict; it's a way of life. That said, conflict is an everyday reality that requires everyday peace. Our discipleship invitation is to be everyday peacemakers who are formed and mobilized to love creatively in our conflicted world. But where does the ideal of peace actually take shape in the realities of everyday life?

Our understanding of Jesus' peacemaking mission—which Paul refers to throughout his letters to the early church—is not merely to bring about "spiritual" peace between God and humanity but to fully restore all creation. This restoration isn't a spiritual transaction but a holistic repair of the relationship among God and humanity and all the created order. As such, our vocation as everyday peacemakers requires us to move into the tangible and everyday realities of life. Jesus described the kingdom of God as a mustard seed: tiny, less than glamorous, and extremely tangible. So we shouldn't be surprised when God's best work unfolds in the mundane realities of everyday life. In a world that glorifies bigger as better, we must wake up to the opportunities to join God in helping these mustard seeds of restoration germinate.

Peacemaking is not reserved to a thirty-thousand-foot ideal nor an aspirational value in the halls of political power. It is not just for the full-time activist. Being a peacemaker is what is means to follow Jesus. It is for the mothers, fathers, brothers, sisters, friends, colleagues, pastors, dishwashers, coaches, and business persons of the world. It is an everyday way of life that occurs in the contexts of our interpersonal relationships, local injustices, and international conflicts.

INTERPERSONAL CONFLICT

As inherently communal creatures, we are shaped by relationship. Whether with our parents, siblings, friends, or spouse, relationships frame our worldview and bring texture, meaning, and richness to our everyday lives. Relationships are also a lot of work, requiring communication, vulnerability, initiative, and inconvenience. We all know relationships take work to be what they were intended to be, but it is often much easier to maintain the status quo through surface-level conversation as a way to protect ourselves from heartache, conflict, and vulnerability.

Further, we are all broken people. No matter how hard we may try not to, we bring our own dysfunction into our relationships, which makes conflict inherent. For these reasons, everyday peacemakers must move toward conflict with those they are closest to. In our experience, this is often the most challenging context for peacemaking. When we talk about international issues, it's easy to leave the conflict "over there" and stay insulated and "safe" from personal implications in our everyday lives. In contrast, interpersonal conflict in our homes, faith communities, and workplaces lets us live out our understanding of peacemaking more holistically.

If we aren't leaning into hard conversations and conflicts with our friends, spouses, and kids, we have no credibility when it comes to teaching others around the country and the world for this work. Disarray in our relationships at home also destabilizes and short-circuits the development of relationships beyond. I (Jon) can think of countless times when my wife and I were at odds—usually over something trivial—and it completely took over my thoughts, emotions, and ability to be fully present with others. Or when I experienced tension with someone in my faith community and started to avoid them or feel anxious about interacting with them. Or when I had a run-in with a colleague and had no choice but to work beside that colleague the very next day.

It might be the family member you've distanced yourself from over the years because of theological or political differences.

It might be the close friend who said something hurtful behind your back that now festers and grows resentment.

It might be the neighbor who constantly antagonizes you over things like parking spots, loud music, or crying children.

It might be the abusive father who has left you with deep trauma that continues to manifest itself in your relationship with your kids.

It might be the coworker who lied about you, leading to your termination and subsequent financial instability.

Whatever the relationship, interpersonal conflict is inevitable and often a reflection of genuine relationship. As John Paul Lederach says, conflict is the most dynamic laboratory for genuine relationship. We don't have any choice but to move toward interpersonal conflict and seek restoration—these are the relationships that offer the stability and foundation for how we live and move in the world.

Finally, how we navigate interpersonal conflict has major implications for the way we bear witness to the Prince of Peace to our neighbors. If our homes, churches, and workplaces are marked by infighting, shallow interactions, and competitive posturing, we no longer reflect the one we follow. The church is to be a sign of who God is and the world he is making by living in mutual submission under his rule and reign.

LOCAL INJUSTICE

Everyday peacemakers are women and men who identify, engage, and seek to participate in transforming the broken systems that are breaking people in their neighborhoods and cities. Our culture makes it easy to see our neighborhoods simply as places to sleep between commutes. But we believe all people have been placed in their unique context for a reason and are called to seek the peace of their city. If we are engaged in achieving peace on the other side of the world without seeking it in our own neighborhood, we have an incomplete and incoherent understanding of what it means to live as everyday peacemakers.

I (Jon) live in the neighborhood of Golden Hill, just outside of downtown San Diego. My family is part of a little faith community whose members have all chosen to live in the same neighborhood as a way to share a common way of life, mission, and play. Our hope is to be a reconciling presence in our neighborhood as a microcosm of the greater reconciliation God made real in Jesus. For us, church isn't a building we attend once a week; it is our neighborhood that we have been called to inhabit, care for, and learn within alongside our neighbors.

A few years ago I helped start the Golden Hill Farmers' Market as a way to support local businesses, promote ethical food consumption, and build community with neighbors. It was remarkable how quickly I was exposed to both the beautiful and broken realities of my neighborhood. Golden Hill has been a majority Latino community for decades, but with an increase in gentrification, the number of Latinos—many of whom are undocumented immigrants—has dropped to about fifty percent. In one sense the farmers' market was a beautiful sign of community and relational space.

In another sense it exposed the fact that our neighborhood is segregated. Almost all the vendors and customers at the market were middle- to upper-class white people who had moved into the neighborhood in recent years and held a high value for ethical consumption. The market was filled with economic, social, and political barriers of entry for our Latino neighbors, and it was expensive, culturally disorienting, and politically unsafe if their documentation status were to be exposed as a result of their participation.

My growing understanding of the history of my city as a border town and my neighborhood as a historic safe haven for immigrants led me to join our neighborhood council. It was an opportunity for me to put my money where my mouth was and help identify local injustice as well as constructively engage the broken systems of gentrification, greed, and racial inequality in my neighborhood. These were systems that both displaced the native Latino community and compromised the security of the local immigrant families. In large part they weren't based on inherent hatred or intentional segregation, which made them even more complex and potentially problematic to confront. Moving into this local injustice as an everyday peacemaker required intentionality, listening, asking lots of hard questions, and, most of all, being present among Golden Hill's residents.

One evening while I was sitting in our council meeting, one of my colleagues proposed turning our little municipal golf course into a semi-private club that would bring in big-money sponsors and wealthy clientele. He spoke for about twenty minutes, casting a vision for how it would benefit real estate values, boost public perception of our historically violent neighborhood, and put us on the map among other "nice" neighborhoods in San Diego. While I could understand where he was coming from, I was shocked by the shortsighted, ethnocentric nature of his proposal.

When he concluded, I knew it was one of those moments when I had to make a choice to lean into potential conflict. I said, "While I understand your perspective, I don't think we should put real estate values above the history and culture of our neighborhood. Many of our neighbors who lived here long before we did have already been pushed out by rising housing costs. If we go forward on this project, we not only compromise the integrity of our leadership; we compromise the long-term presence of the very community whose culture, history, and presence make Golden Hill what it is."

Sadly, my perspective was the minority, which is also why it was important. When we move toward local injustice as everyday peacemakers, we must be intentional, present, and willing to be misunderstood and ridiculed for the sake of sticking a fork in the spokes of injustice. Broken systems are breaking people in our neighborhoods, and we are called toward them as a presence of reconciliation.

INTERNATIONAL CONFLICT

We live in a world where our local actions send ripples around the globe, for good or bad. At the same time, conflict on the other side of the world affects our cities and neighborhoods, whether through heightened security protocols or increased numbers of refugee families who are fleeing violence. Further, as citizens of the USA, we are part of a political superpower that directly impacts policy and everyday life for people around the world. We have to take our international influence seriously and understand ourselves to be part of an interdependent global family. We have to embrace our dual citizenship in the United States and the kingdom of God with savvy, clarity, and conviction. We must always understand our citizenship in the kingdom of God as primary, while simultaneously leveraging our citizenship in the Unites States to promote just policy and presence internationally. In 2016, we witnessed one of the worst refugee crises in the history of humanity as women, men, and children fled the violence that swept through their villages in Syria and Iraq. The rise of the so-called Islamic state destabilized the region, and Western airstrikes shook the foundations of everyday life. Hundreds of these precious human beings drowned after being forced by smugglers onto boats that weren't fit for the open waters of the Mediterranean. We are fathers, and seeing kids as young as ours being pulled from the rough seas without the light of life in their eyes breaks our hearts and has forced us to choose between paralysis and peacemaking.

As everyday peacemakers, we need to speak boldly to political power players and remind them of their opportunity to pursue human flourishing and restoration. As this crisis builds, there is a growing narrative being told throughout the United States that if we offer refuge to these families fleeing violence, we make ourselves vulnerable to terrorist attacks on our own soil. As a result, fear is trumping invitation and a frenzy of paranoia and paralysis is strangling our ability to see the humanity, dignity, and image of God in the world's most vulnerable. Whether it is a refugee crisis or any number of other broken realities that continue to grow in our world, the truth is that we may expose ourselves to violence when we care for those in need. But Jesus didn't invite us into a life of safety—he invited us to be faithful.

Prioritizing safety over faithfulness leads to a life of entrenchment rather than invitation. In an entrenched, defensive faith, fear trumps hope, isolation trumps invitation, stereotype trumps understanding, dogma trumps generosity, critique trumps curiosity, and, ultimately, hate trumps love.

Bordering countries in the Middle East and Europe are taking in refugees by the hundreds of thousands and the United States has struggled to approve twelve thousand despite our extreme wealth, high-tech security, and robust vetting systems. Lebanon, a nation of six million, has welcomed over one million Syrian refugees, and over twenty-five percent of Jordan's population is now made up of refugees from conflict zones. In order for the church to be the church and care for the least of these, everyday peacemakers must speak truth to power and charge them to open up our national doors so we can welcome the stranger in our midst.

Most importantly, our role as everyday peacemakers in international conflict often happens most effectively through local practice. While we probably won't personally broker a peace agreement in Syria, we can certainly walk with Syrian refugees by partnering with local resettlement agencies and "adopting" a family. While we probably won't be personally responsible for restored relationship between Israel and Palestine, we can educate our churches and ourselves by pursuing diverse media sources, identifying unhelpful theology that contributes to the conflict, and building relationships with local Muslims and Jews who are tied to the region. Whatever the international conflict, our engagement locally can have helpful or harmful implications for our sisters and brothers around the world.

THE OPPORTUNITY OF EVERYDAY PEACEMAKING

If you asked our kids what we do for work, their answer would be simple: "Our daddy teaches peacemaking." For them, being a peacemaker is their highest aspiration. We talk about it on the way to school, pray about it before bed, and discuss it throughout the day. In their little kid worlds, peacemaking looks like making everyone in their class feel welcome and included. Or always saying hello to their neighbors. Or helping mom and dad with their younger siblings (we *really* emphasize this one!). In its simplicity, peacemaking is beautiful and tangible. It is saturating their understanding of Jesus' invitation to live lives of love everywhere, every day.

Whether we're choosing to read bedtime stories that reflect diversity and inclusion or inviting our kids to accompany us into the beautiful and broken realities of our city and nation, we believe the formation of our children is the most important work we've been given.

Near the end of my (Jon's) daughter Ruby's preschool year, they had "career day." Of course, Ruby lit up and volunteered me to come in to share about my work as a peacemaker. Honestly, I hadn't been this nervous about a speaking engagement in a long time. I could speak to forty-year-old academics or pastors all day long, but a room full of three- and four-year-olds? I anticipated it'd be rough—and it was.

Ruby introduced me in her bashful but proud way and I took the stage. I opened by saying, "My name is Jon and I'm a peacemaker." Their eyes lit up with excitement and I started to feel pretty good about myself. Then in unison they yelled, "He's a pizza maker!" My greatest fears were being realized.

We did some skits on the stage to illustrate what peacemaking could look like at school, at home, and at the park. Just as I was thinking I had clarified their misunderstanding and made a solid case for peacemaking, one little fella came up to me and whispered, "I like pepperoni."

While I may not have won the day with these three- and four-year-olds, I couldn't have been more proud of Ruby's genuine joy to share the good news of peacemaking with her friends. We have a sacred opportunity and responsibility to invite our kids into this way of life at an early age. As we discussed in the last chapter, there are theological, social, and political barriers that can hijack our ability to gain a theology and practice of peacemaking in our culture. The time is now for us to save the next generation decades of "unlearning" all the poor theology around peacemaking and accompany them in adopting a life and practice of peacemaking as central to their understanding of Jesus.

While everyday peacemaking gives our immediate families the sacred opportunity to reflect the Prince of Peace locally, it also lets us identify ourselves as part of an interdependent kingdom family that extends from our doorstep to the other side of the world and back again.

As I shared in chapter one, my brief interaction with a Christian Palestinian man from the West Bank village of Bethany upended my worldview, theology, and heart in the best ways possible. This man, Milad, and his remarkable wife, Manar, have become two of our primary guides and teachers in the costly, subversive, and everyday work of peace. In the same way Lazarus was resurrected in Bethany two thousand years ago, resurrection is taking place on the modern streets of Bethany as a result of their faithfulness today. Each time we bring a Global Immersion delegation to Israel/Palestine, we sit in their backyard to learn from them.

Milad grew up on the narrow streets of Jerusalem in the Middle East, and we grew up on the beaches of California and icy lakes of Wisconsin. We are similar ages but have experienced completely different versions of history. As fathers, our everyday lives are extremely similar, but as inhabitants of different regions of the world, they are nothing alike. Despite endless differences, our souls are one and our commitment to following Jesus, crossing borders, and participating in God's peace unites us in a way we've never experienced. At the conclusion of one of our trips to Bethany, Milad and Manar presented us with an engraved plaque they called the "Brothers of Peace" award.

Alejandra Ortiz and Abdiel Espinoza live in Tijuana, Mexico, just fifteen miles south of my neighborhood in San Diego. They work with an organization called Compa. In one sense we are neighbors, but in another they live a world apart. The majority of our neighbors to the south live a vastly different life from those of us in the United States. Ale and Abdiel live at the intersection of these two worlds, speaking prophetically to the political and religious elite of their city on behalf of the migrant population that is abused, exploited, and forgotten by those with power and influence.

While they are some of our primary guides and instructors for the work of peace, they have also become our dear friends. The more we share our hearts and our lives, the more we understand the value of building interdependent friendships that cross our inherited borders and boundaries. Over the years they have taught us much about our call to peacemaking and, in turn, they have leaned in and learned from my little church community about the importance of sharing life, mission, and play in a specific neighborhood as a presence of reconciliation. In fact, a few months ago they asked me (and a couple of others from my community) to help them launch a sister church community in Tijuana. Two different countries, two different cities, two different cultures, but two communities that are intimately linked in their commitment to one another and to living the peacemaking way of Jesus. What an opportunity we have to join in the global work God is doing.

The intersection of these two couples—and the two worlds they represent—happened in my backyard. For the first time in their lives Milad and Manar were able to get visas to visit the United States, and when I told Ale and Abdiel that they'd be at our house for an intimate event to share about their work for peace in the West Bank, their response was, "We want to meet them!" On a warm night in May, friends and colleagues from Mexico crossed an international border. Global Immersion alumni flew from the other side of the country. Neighbors walked directly across the street. Our whole church community in Golden Hill leaned in. And our friends and mentors from the West Bank shared about their work, which is sowing seeds of hope, life, and peace in the most prophetic and provocative ways imaginable.

We listened. We laughed. We learned. We danced (a lot). Our kids were right in the middle of the action and stayed up way too late. We celebrated the gift of relationship that transcends inherited borders and boundaries. If I were asked what the kingdom of God is like, I'd start by describing that evening. These experiences give us front row seats to witness the world God is making. A world I want my kids to taste and know they can be part of ushering in.

Near the end of our time together, Milad decided to name his backyard "Golden Hill Garden" in honor of our neighborhood, and I committed to calling our backyard "Bethany Garden" for his West Bank neighborhood. The life that animates and fills his home is the same that fills ours. As kingdom family, we live interdependent lives that remind us of our shared humanity and flourishing.

This is the opportunity before each one of us. When we say yes to the call to live as everyday peacemakers amid interpersonal conflict, local injustice, and international discord, we will be invited into uncommon friendships that transcend both physical borders and the boundaries of our imagination for what God has in mind for our world. May we take seriously our call to everyday peacemaking and wake up to the gift of being part of an interdependent kingdom family that is joining in God's mission of reconciliation.

REFLECT AND DISCUSS

1. Have you considered the life of peacemaking as discipleship? Why or why not?

2. What are some ways you continue to adhere to a pseudo-discipleship that contributes to a false identity, short-circuits formation, and compromises a cross-shaped witness?

3. What personal relationship in your life needs mending?

4. What local conflict do you feel compelled to engage? Which international conflict compels you?

FIVE

SEE

Seek the Peace is a one-of-a-kind organization strategically placed within the underresourced refugee community of Dallas, Texas. It's founded and led by our friend and fellow peacemaker Jason Clarke (see seekingpeace.org). The neighborhood Seek serves is currently home to ten thousand refugees from fifteen countries who speak 140 different languages. Most of them fled trauma to get there. All of them endured years-long vetting processes.

After six hours of training Seek the Peace staff members in the everyday realities of peacemaking, we shifted from theory to practice out necessity. As we drove from the office, the local high school was letting out and the streets were filling with young people from all over the world. We pulled up to a stoplight and found ourselves immersed in the middle of a street fight between young Burmese and West African refugees who wielded nunchucks, Tasers, and aluminum baseball bats. These were the violent few of Jason's neighborhood that most people refused to see.

Without hesitation Jason threw his car into park and ran into the center of the fray, armed not with weapons but with tools of transformation. In a matter of minutes, a fight that could have sealed the fate of many dissipated and the warring parties began to step down.

As the fight de-escalated, we looked around to discover lines of cars backed up as far as we could see filled with gawking adults ignoring the traffic lights. Two police cars edged by, the policemen casting seemingly indifferent glances in our direction. Hundreds of kids stood paralyzed, prepared to watch one more bloodbath in the violent streets of their neighborhood. And then we saw Jason, still in the middle of the road, arms outstretched, looking into the eyes of those hurting kids.

While many people saw violence that day, Jason saw humanity. He saw their dignity and God's image imprinted on each one of them. He saw their plight and their pain. What Jason saw that afternoon stopped him dead in his tracks.

Everyday peacemakers are men and women who see the humanity, dignity, and image of God in all people. They see the pain of others and they understand their own contributions to the injustice around them.

Seeing is our first peacemaking practice.

THE GOOD SAMARITAN

There's a poignant story in the Gospel of Luke that has stood the test of time. It's regarded by people of all faiths as a story that reveals the very best and worst of humanity. The parable is named after the protagonist, a "Good Samaritan" who helped an abused victim alongside a dangerous road. As riveting as the story is—and continues to be each time it's told and retold—it is also an answer given by Jesus in response to an important question by a real person.

The questioner was a young Pharisee who at first sought insight into how he could be in community with God and his friends for eternity. It was an excellent question, but he was a scholar and already knew the correct answer: "'Love the Lord your God with all your heart and with all your soul and with all your strength and with all your mind'; and, 'Love your neighbor as yourself'" (Luke 10:27). Almost dismissively, Jesus affirmed the young lawyer's knowledge and encouraged him to live out these two critical teachings of the Torah.

But there was something else the young man was digging for, so he asked a follow-up question: "And who is my neighbor?" (Luke 10:29). This inquiry was fueled not by a sacrificial desire to love all humanity but was myopic and self-serving. The real question being asked was: "Who am I obligated to see and who am I allowed to ignore?"

Understanding the question behind the question, Jesus answered by telling a controversial story. "The Good Samaritan" was and is a masterfully told parable about crime, violence, racism, injustice, mercy, and compassion. It is a marvelous story in which Jesus chose to identify someone outside his own people group and faith tradition to exemplify a faithful life. A contemporary comparison might be if a well-known pastor offered a Syrian Muslim refugee, an undocumented Latino migrant, or an HIV-infected transgendered woman as an example of what it means to faithfully follow Jesus.

The story Jesus told both answered the lawyer's question and exposed the peacemaking heart and activity of God. Its impact went even further, though, as it offered an invitation to the lawyer, those who listened then, and those who listen today to go and live likewise.

THE JERICHO ROAD TRAVELER
AND THE VIOLENT FEW

The story began with a man walking the dangerous, seventeen-mile Jericho road while a group of people hid and waited for an unsuspecting victim. The traveler "was attacked by robbers. They stripped him of his clothes, beat him and went away, leaving him half dead" (Luke 10:30). As blood saturated the dirt road, the predators made away with the man's belongings only to regroup, count their spoils, and likely do it again and again and again.

Before moving too quickly toward the grand entrances of the priest and Levite, let's wonder for a bit about the lives of these violent few. Who were they? What neighborhoods did they come from? What experiences pushed them to the wilderness where they spent their lives hiding behind rocks and overwhelming travelers with violence? What were the systems in place that had robbed their hope, calcified their imaginations, and interrupted their ability to see the humanity, dignity, and image of God in others? Did they show preference for particular kinds of people or was their violence completely unbiased? Did they steal for sport or because it was the only way they could survive? Had anyone ever offered them the opportunity to heal? Had anyone ever offered them a different alternative to violence and robbery?

These questions usually go unasked when we explore this particular story. They also go unasked when we hear of or experience conflict, pain, and violence of any kind in the world around us. Instead we tend to group "dangerous" people together, categorize them as "violent," and believe our own conclusions. We distance ourselves from them and rarely if ever dignify them with our curiosity. Neither do we consider the ways in which we have participated in forming and benefiting from the systems that have caused these people to live in the shadows and enact violence to survive.

Yes, this particular group of human beings chose violence over human decency. Rather than seeing the humanity, dignity, and image of God in Jericho road travelers, they saw objects that they could exploit.

ENTER THE RELIGIOUS ELITE

The story continues with the arrival of the religious elite to the site of the violence. Jesus continued, "A priest happened to be going down the same road, and when he saw the man, he passed by on the other side. So too, a Levite, when he came to the place and saw him, passed by on the other side" (Luke 10:31-32).

The priest, on his way home from performing his religious duties at the temple in Jerusalem, was first on the scene. In Jerusalem he had likely offered sacrifices on behalf of Israel's sins. Simply put, his sacrificial work was supposed to enable Israel to live out its vocation as a people of blessing to foreigners, the marginalized, the exploited, and the misunderstood. On this particular day, his work completed, he was returning home to Jericho when he stumbled upon a voiceless victim on a broken road.

What the priest noticed that day no doubt raised a series of questions that would have created a dilemma for him. *Is this an ambush? Am I the next voiceless victim? Is this person a deserved sinner? Did he have it coming to him? Is he a Gentile or, God forbid, a Samaritan? Is he already dead? What will happen to me, my ability to perform my religious duties, and my reputation among the religious elite if I choose compassion over indifference?*

The questions led to conclusions that informed the priest's action. Distracted by his desire to return home and remain faithful, he chose to cross by on the other side of the road and ignore the broken life in front of him. His understanding of religious faithfulness stymied his compassion. Fear of disqualification and a soiled reputation won the day. His religious understanding of serving God interrupted his ability to see and respond to the pain he had stumbled on.

So too a Levite entered the story. He traveled the same road and, like the priest, happened on the man left for dead. A similar set of questions would have emerged for the Levite, causing him to also notice rather than see the voiceless victim.

Before moving too quickly into a critique of the religious elite, we should note that they often get some unfair treatment in our readings of this story. In first-century Judaism, ritual purity was of paramount importance to members of the religious community, who acted as mediators between God and the people. For them, ritual purity or "cleanliness" was central to remaining faithful to God and the unique vocation they had been entrusted with. If they compromised their cleanliness, even if it meant walking by a dying human being, they could compromise the well-being of the greater community of God they were called to represent. It's not that they were trying to be bad people; they were simply trying to be faithful people. We can imagine them asking the question, "To which am I more responsible: the dying man on the side of road or the well-being of the larger community God has called me to represent?"

We might think we are in a position where caring for the dying man and the larger community aren't mutually exclusive, but it's not as clear as we might initially think. We can't point our collective finger at the unfaithfulness of the religious elite without first evaluating our understanding of faithfulness. How often do we avoid those who are different from us or who act in ways we see as "sinful" because we are concerned that they or their actions might taint our faithfulness? Or, asked another way, how often do we consider how our associations could compromise our witness, reputation, or orthodoxy?

To the shock of those listening to this story, Jesus placed the religious elite in the same camp as the violent few. Both groups failed to see the humanity, dignity, and image of God in the voiceless victim. While the violent few saw him as an exploitable object, the religious elite saw him as a compromising inconvenience.

The blood from a slow, lonely, agonizing death was on the hands of both the violent and the religious.

THE PROBLEM OF DAMAGED SIGHT

Something had damaged the priest's and Levite's ability to see this person as a human being. What was it?

Was it an elevated sense of call or personal importance?

Was it lifelong patterns of busyness and fulfilling an overly full schedule?

Was it their understanding of what faithfulness required of them?

Was it opinions, fears, and biases that had been ingrained into them through their upbringing? Had they heard and told stories, even jokes, about the Jericho road and the kinds of people who got in trouble there?

Let's make this a bit more personal. What about us? What has damaged our ability to see the humanity, dignity, and image of God in other people? What are the variables that blind us from seeing people whose lives are different or broken? What inhibits us from seeing the pain of those closest to us?

Is it our own sense of personal importance? Do we live by an unspoken cultural caste system that helps us identify who does and doesn't deserve our time, touch, and attention?

How does the frenetic pace of our lives and our calendars blind us to what is beautiful and broken around us?

What opinions, fears, and biases have been ingrained in us through our upbringing, the brand of church we've been a part of, and our preferred media sources?

We, like the violent few and the religious elite of Jesus' story, have been trained to see and to not see certain people. The people we are most concerned about tend to be a homogenous, insulated few. We're very clear who the "us" and the "them" are, and we are careful to keep the distinction defined and the distance severe.

To help with this, we tell each other stories in which we play the heroes and "others" are the villains. We speak of our "others" not as different but as wrong, dangerous, violent, and to be feared. We trust only those who think, believe, sound, and act like us and grow progressively suspicious of accents, skin tones, economic disparities, sexual orientations, political affiliations, and names of God that are different from ours. We manage our fear not by seeing them, building friendships, or allowing them to teach us about who they are but by not seeing them at all.

ENTER THE "GOOD" SAMARITAN

Returning to the story Jesus told, the voiceless victim is still lying alone and unconscious on a violent road. The young lawyer and those listening were hanging on the words of Jesus and waiting anxiously to see what would happen next. With three words, the story took a dramatic twist. "But a Samaritan . . . " (Luke 10:33).

Had Jesus stopped there, the consensus of the crowd would have been that this new character was being introduced to finish the job begun by the violent few. From a Jewish perspective, Samaritans were half-breeds with a tainted religion. They were despised, subhuman neighbors who were incapable of compassion and to be avoided at all costs. Surely a representative of this immoral people would enact violence on the victim.

Contrary to these expectations, Jesus elevated the Samaritan as the only one who refused to let racial or religious barriers hinder him from truly seeing the victim. Keep in mind what it was the Samaritan saw. He saw a broken human being who wore no clothes and thus carried no tribal identification. He saw an unconscious victim who couldn't be identified by language, dialect, or accent. While the victim was nothing but a bruised canvas, the Samaritan saw the humanity, dignity, and image of God in this broken life.

This was the climax of the story. Jesus had just exposed the tendency of those in the listening crowd to misunderstand and reject people from different tribes and traditions as wrong and dangerous. By including this one foreign character, Jesus invited his listeners and us to see God at work in the lives of those we would deem unorthodox, heretical, or of different faith traditions.

Through his story of the compassionate Samaritan, Jesus invites us to look at those we've chosen not to see. He demands that we see them, for in so doing we will be stunned by what we discover about who God is, what God is like, and who God is for. When we see the unconventional, those we've marginalized and misunderstood, as collaborators of peace, we will begin to humanize them.

Jesus invited the lawyer, the listening crowd, and those of us today to look at the Samaritan and discover what it means to love and to be loved by our enemy.

Do you hear the heart of God in this? We are the voiceless victims lying alone on a blood-soaked road. Our God saw our humanity. He saw our dignity. He saw his image in us. Ours is a God who saw our conflict-riddled story, our shattered reality, and our pain-induced plight. We have a God who saw our terminal disease and how we suffered because of it. Remarkably, what God saw neither caused him to sidestep us nor turn and walk away. Instead, what God saw stopped him dead in his tracks and became the most important thing in the world to him.

Everyday peacemakers are men and women who choose to see the humanity, dignity, and image of God in others and who understand the plight of the voiceless. We are people who choose to see our own biases, opinions, lies, and fears as well as our contributions to what is broken around us. We are men and women who acknowledge our blindness, understand what has contributed to it, and ask God to heal our sight.

JESUS, THE SIGHT-HEALER

Of Jesus' thirty-one miracles documented in the Gospels, nearly one in four involves the healing of sight. The abundance of miracles involving the restoration of sight communicates something of the spiritual awakening that the life, death, and resurrection of Jesus would bring to the world. Let's look at four of the better-known sight healings of Jesus and distill from them what his healing looked like then and looks like now.

First is the blind man in Bethsaida who saw walking trees (Mark 8:22-26). As the story goes, a group of friends had heard that Jesus had the authority to heal the untreatable. They longed for the unthinkable to happen to their blind friend. So they brought him to Jesus who, instead of healing him in the presence of many, led him by the hand outside of the city, spit in his eyes, and asked him what he saw. The man, who was no longer blind replied, "I see people, but they're like walking trees." Jesus touched his eyes again, and this time the man's sight was fully restored.

There were also two blind men in Capernaum who identified Jesus as the fulfillment of messianic prophecy (Matthew 9:27-31). If their hunch about Jesus was accurate, they knew the healing of sight would accompany his presence (Isaiah 61). They were desperate for their hunch to be validated, so they cried out for mercy. Jesus heard their cries and, instead of immediately healing their sight, asked them if they believed he could do it. When they told him they believed, he touched their eyes and they could see.

Another blind man was the only one in the crowd to accurately identify Jesus as the Son of David (Luke 18:35-43; Mark 10:46-52; Matthew 20:29-34). Ignoring the attempts to silence him, the blind man cried out for Jesus' attention. This was his chance and he was desperate. As the event unfolded, Jesus heard the man's cries and was undeterred by the attempts of his community to pass the man by.

Jesus drew near the blind man. Only this time he asked an ironic question: "What do you want me to do for you?" Wasn't it obvious? Jesus was looking into eyes that carried no sight. Unshaken, the man replied, "Lord, I want to see!" An ironic question received a very specific answer. That answer revealed both the man's desperation and his faith, so Jesus again gave the gift of sight to the blind.

In our final episode, a Jerusalem-born blind man had been kicked to the fringes of society under the assumption that his blindness was either a result of his or his family's sin (John 9:1-12, 35-37). Jesus' own disciples embodied the cultural prejudice when they walked by, noticed his blindness, and asked Jesus about his sin problem. Jesus, on the other hand, didn't just notice the man. He saw the blind man, and what he saw became the most important thing in the world to him.

Unlike the first three events, Jesus' healing in this case wasn't overtly asked for. And unlike in times past, this time Jesus made a mess before he did the miraculous. He spat on the ground, mixed the very DNA of God with the dirt, put the mud in the blind man's eyes, and told him to go wash it out. Once the blind man rinsed the mud from his eyes, his sight was restored.

According to these accounts, Jesus was and is actively invested in restoring sight to the blind. If we're to take these stories seriously, it seems as though sight-healing happens in odd and intimate ways. In some cases the healing requires faith and takes time, while in other cases the immediacy of the healing surprises us. Some healings require a community of friends believing in the touch of Jesus and bringing us to him. Others involve a different substance than what we might have preferred.

What if, like so many of those healed by Jesus, we owned our blindness and made it a practice to cry out, "I want to see like you see"? What if we acknowledged that the systems we were raised in taught us to see and not see certain groups of people? What if we confessed our preference for particular media channels and worked to understand how a steady diet of them had formed cataracts in our eyes and blurred our sight? What if we analyzed our upbringing to discover where our mentors' biases scratched the corneas of our souls, causing damage to our ability to see particular people with generosity and empathy? If we want to see like God sees, we need to do the hard work of understanding what caused our blindness and then cry out for the healing touch of Jesus.

When we pray that prayer, an essential journey from noticing to seeing begins. On that journey we find ourselves aware of things we've never seen before. We become people who choose to see things that make us uncomfortable. What we see begins to change us and produce compassion in us. That compassion, the precursor to responsibility, propels us forward to become a part of just solutions that lead to restoration.

HEALED SIGHT IN TIJUANA

In the last chapter we introduced Alejandra Ortiz, a subversive prophet and embedded peacemaking practitioner who is a true example of what happens when Jesus heals our sight. A native of Tijuana, Ale has committed her life to discipling student leaders. However, as happens so frequently among dynamic faith leaders, her work developing students in their faith had blinded her from seeing the plight of the migrants and deportees in her own neighborhood.

While Tijuana is a stunning city with one of the strongest economies in Mexico, it is one of many cosmopolitan centers throughout the world trying to figure out what to do with a surplus of migrants and deportees. Growing up in this city, Ale had heard stories about the people who hid in the shadows and had even noticed their presence in the streets. Her heart naturally bent toward the marginalized and the misunderstood, but it wasn't until her discipleship required her to become a student of her city that Jesus began to heal her sight.

As Ale learned the history of Tijuana, Jesus began to help her move beyond noticing to seeing the humanity, dignity, and image of God in the deportees. Her formation shifted from "learning about" to "learning from" as she built authentic friendships with people on the move. What Ale saw generated compassion in her, and she dared to pray that God would open a door so that she could become a part of restoration.

Quicker than she expected, her prayer was answered. She received an invitation to join a filmmaker who was working on a documentary. Sex tourism was the focus of the film—due to its proximity to San Diego, Tijuana is considered the Bangkok of Latin America. The filmmaker wanted access to one club in particular, and he asked Ale if she would come along to help translate. The door opened and Ale walked through it into the most insidious neighborhood in Tijuana. She followed Jesus to the place where migration and human trafficking collide and where the dreams of college boys create a nightmare for those trapped in an international red-light district.

While in the club Ale met a young woman who owed a massive debt to the owner. Maria was a migrant and mother of one who had come to Tijuana to pursue opportunity for her family. Unfortunately, like so many others, she had stumbled on hard times and needed lodging and food for two. The club offered the support she needed, all the while keeping tabs on her expenses. It wasn't until she was ready to move on that she discovered how massive her debt was to the club and learned how the debt was to be paid.

Maria had been paying off her debt through sex shifts in the club for more than a year when Ale met her. Rather than seeing her as dirty and labeling her a prostitute, Ale saw the image of God in Maria. She saw her humanity, beauty, dignity, and potential. She saw her pain, her crushed dreams, and her decimated identity. She learned of Maria's son, her goal to open her own salon, and the pain and shame involved in paying off an unending debt. Over time Maria and Ale have developed a significant yet complicated friendship through which hope is growing, the debt is dissipating, and Maria's identity and dignity are being restored.

Today Ale continues to form and mobilize emerging leaders. Only now she does so by inviting them to join her in seeing the humanity, dignity, and image of God in the forgotten and oppressed in her own neighborhood.

BECOMING EVERYDAY PEACEMAKERS WHO SEE

So how do we, a people seen by God, become everyday peacemakers who see? Here are six simple actions that we can take this week to increase our capacity to see.

First, like the blind men who knew the authority Jesus held and cried out for sight, we can pray and ask the great sight-healer to help us embrace the beautiful reality that we are seen and cherished by him. We can pray that he would continue to heal our sight such that we begin to see ourselves and others—the beautiful and the broken—as he sees them.

Second, we can enter into the often-neglected ancient practice of lament. The sin and brokenness in our own lives functions like acid to the eyes of our soul, marring our ability to see the truth about God, ourselves, and others. We need to learn how to pause and acknowledge the pain we've caused others, whether intentionally or unintentionally. At the same time we need to learn to mourn what is broken and unjust around us as well as mourn with those who suffer as a result. We need to learn to hate the injustice, confess our complicity, repent of it, learn from it, and work to ensure that restoration occurs. If and when we get to experience restoration, we should be zealous to celebrate that it no longer holds destructive, blinding power over us nor over those caught up in the pain.

Third, we can repent of our vehement commitment to our own personal flourishing. Like cataracts in our eyes, self-preference and the idolatry of "me" render our sight useless. Repentance requires careful, prayerful reflection, acknowledgment, and movement in the opposite direction, which results in a steadily clarifying perspective. We encourage emerging peacemakers to seek contemplative solitude with a trusted few and ask these questions:

1. How does my sense of personal importance hinder my ability to see what is beautiful and broken around me?

2. What are the opinions, biases, and prejudices that have been ingrained in me through my upbringing, brand of church, and preferred media sources?

3. Am I too busy to see the humanity, dignity, and image of God in those I love, live with, stumble into, and work alongside?

Fourth, like Ale, we can allow research to become a part of our discipleship. To do this, we must first become students of the people around us and learn to ask better questions: What makes them come alive? What do they want to accomplish in their lifetime? What holds them back? What were the moments and who were the people that most shaped them?

We should also utilize historical resources in our cities to learn the story of our place. Who were the indigenous people? Where did they go? What is the good, bad, and ugly of your city today and how has that been informed by its history?

Fifth, we can put our screens away, slow down, and pay attention. It is simply amazing what we miss because we spend our idle time looking at a screen instead of into the eyes of those around us. If we're praying for healed sight and opened doors, then when we slow down and look up, we will see beautiful and broken things we've never seen before. We should keep a running note of what we notice and allow ourselves to be moved by what we see.

Sixth, we can pursue relationships. As was the case with Jason and Ale, authentic relationships set the context for our sight to improve. It's through relationship that God finds us, forms us, and heals our sight. We need to stop walking by people and start leveraging our lunch hours, our front porches, and our dinner tables to build friendships. Further, it's helpful to identify the people in our lives who are excellent at seeing the beauty and the broken around them. We should pursue them, sit with them, and learn from them.

This week, let's take a neighborhood walk. As we go, let's ask God to help us see the things he would have us see in that moment. Chances are good that while we look around, God will be inviting us to look within.

Some of what we see, both internally an externally, will be beautiful and some of it will be broken. When it's possible, we can take a photo. Perhaps we will see something stunning in our neighborhood. Maybe we'll see something externally that moves us to see our own internal beauty or brokenness more deeply. Let's capture it so we can keep seeing what God needs us to see. There's a chance God will reveal an issue of injustice, pain, or brokenness in our neighborhood through art, a dilapidated building, or a billboard. We can take a picture of it and use that

photo as a tool for the Spirit to further awaken us to the plight
of those around us.

REFLECT AND DISCUSS

1. Where do you find yourself in the story about Jason and the
   street fight? Distanced gawker? Paralyzed observer? Indifferent passerby? Immersed peacemaker? What are the experiences, perceptions, or misconceptions that have informed your
   level of engagement?

2. Who have you been taught (or been given permission) *not*
   to see?

3. What obstacles prevent you from seeing the pain and plight
   of others?

4. What is the dangerous dream that you dream about the flourishing of others? How are you joining God in seeing that
   dream come true?

SIX

IMMERSE

There is a major divide between the church and the LGBTQ community in my (Jon's) city. Generally speaking, the church in San Diego feels threatened by the LGBTQ community and believes it needs to defend itself based on its theological and moral convictions, while the LGBTQ community often feels excluded and judged by the church. Interestingly, in the midst of this polarizing reality, my neighborhood rec center has been the home of the NGBA, or the National Gay Basketball Association.

When I first observed the division between the church and the LGBTQ community in San Diego, I lamented its existence but had no idea I how could contribute to collapsing the divide. Honestly, I was paralyzed by the gravity of the disintegration, so I just began to ask some simple questions:

What is the source of the division?

What fear exists within both communities that has led to seeing each other as the "other" rather than as friend?

What experiences have led to the fear and physical division?

Where natural spaces of overlap already exist where I could simply join in as a way to listen, learn, and build friendship?

What will it cost me and how will it impact my reputation if I draw near to my LGBTQ neighbors?

Confronting my own insecurity and fear, and holding true to a core conviction, I chose to lean in alongside a few trusted friends rather than go it alone.

Loving basketball and our neighborhood and knowing the divide between these two communities, a few of us in my little neighborhood church community asked if we could be invited to play in the National Gay Basketball Association (NGBA). We were welcomed with open arms, new friendships were birthed, and, over time and in small ways, the distance between us and the LGBTQ community began to lessen.

Amazing things happen when we move toward and build relationships with people we've only "known" from a distance. Proximity to the "other" matters; it reshapes our worldview, restores our humanity, and tills the soil for collaborative relationship.

For me and for others involved in our league, stigmas were confronted, stereotypes shed, and perceptions replaced with reality. "They" became "us."

One day, while I was playing in our midweek open gym with neighbors and members of the NGBA league, one of my Christian friends yelled, "Hey, Jon, you're not in that gay league, are you?"

He said it in a tone of judgment and disgust in front of my gay teammates. Because I knew his question was one of condemnation and because many of my gay friends were within earshot, I was furious. I jogged over to him, told him I was very much part of the NGBA league and asked him why he wasn't.

He said, "As a Christian, I could never support them."

I responded, "No matter where we land on the LGBTQ issue, as a Christian, I can't imagine a more important community for me to be in relationship with." Knowing I was a pastor, he was thrown off guard and quickly changed the subject.

I went to my friends in the NGBA league and explained to them that not all Christians think and act like my friend who yelled across the gym. Because I was in real relationship with them, they trusted me. The pain of the moment dissipated.

While we wish stories like this weren't true or necessary, they are. There is an unfounded fear in many Christian circles perpetuating the lie that our faith is somehow compromised by spending time and building relationships with people who think, act, or believe differently than we do. We mistakenly believe that if we associate with these people, they will lead us down the slippery slope of compromise.

Isolating ourselves from difference and disagreement doesn't reflect a strong faith but a fragile one. Often, the "other" isn't the problem, but our inability to trust in a God who transcends our perceived borders and boundaries. When we move toward people who are "different" from us, it doesn't compromise our faith; it reflects the very best of it. In fact, it was when I released my need to be understood or affirmed by fellow Christians that I was freed up to live more like Jesus.

The religious elite in Luke 10 found themselves in a similar situation—they chose to see an obstacle to their faith rather than an opportunity to live into it. Like we often do, they got stuck in a dualistic faith that forced them into a corner where they had to choose either faithfulness or compromise. Their understanding of the God life was limited to the boundaries of religiosity. It didn't include the people Jesus said were at the center of the kingdom he was bringing about. Their faith like ours, needed a renovation that would move them toward the "other" rather than around them or away from them.

In the Samaritan, Jesus uses the "unclean" to define what true cleanliness looks like. When our own self-righteousness keeps us from getting our fingers dirty, we lose the opportunity to experience cleanliness and full participation in the world God is making.

JESUS' INCARNATION AS FAITHFUL IMMERSION

God's movement toward conflict with the intention to redeem and transform is no more tangible than in the life of Jesus and his incarnation into our human neighborhood. As the people of God struggled to remain faithful to their vocation as peacemakers who were to bless the world on behalf of God rather than walk away, God saw their plight and chose to immerse into the center of their conflict-riddled story.

Since the time of God's first invitation of Abraham to live as a representative of God's mission of peace, Israel struggled to remain faithful. The lure of power, wealth, and security captured their hearts and imaginations, and they missed the opportunity to mediate between God and humanity, instead submitting themselves to the very things they were intended to redeem. As a result they fell into exile under Assyria, then Babylon. Finally, they found themselves living under the heavy weight of Roman occupation.

It was into this context that God immersed into the human neighborhood in Jesus. God didn't descend to earth as a military leader on the white horse of the Roman Empire who would finally offer the fatal blow to the "enemy" but as a baby born in complete vulnerability.

Inherent in the posture of immersion is vulnerability. God, in Jesus, made himself fully reliant on the care of the ragtag human family he was born into. He didn't insulate or isolate himself from the broken reality of humanity but chose a posture of interdependence on the humanity he came to restore. Stanley Hauerwas says, "God would rather have God's own Son die, than to redeem the world through violence." Jesus didn't enter the world as a war hero. He immersed as a helpless child.

How often do we enter conflict in the posture of a hero rather than of vulnerability and curiosity?

We think this point is especially important since the North American church throughout history has spent more time using religion to colonize and control than to bless and support. We acknowledge that we are part of this tradition. For many of us, our only experience with the majority world has been when it has been on the receiving end of our charity during a traditional short-term mission trip. As well-intentioned as these experiences may be, they have been proven to be part of a broken system that short-circuits the development of sustainable, mutually beneficial relationships. Immersion is not dispensing goods and services while remaining disconnected from relationships with those we're seeking to serve.

Metaphorically, we might raise a bunch of money and offer brain surgeries to hurting people across the world (again, with the best intentions). We fill our newsletters with stories of smiling faces and a genuine sense of accomplishment. Then one of the hurting people gets our attention and says, "Thanks for the brain surgery, but all I needed was a bandage for my scratched knee." In that moment we realize that not only did we fail to give this hurting person what they actually needed; they ended up worse off than before we came—recovery from brain surgery doesn't happen overnight.

One of our Mexican friends, Gilberto, works tirelessly for the flourishing of his deported brothers and sisters in Tijuana. He recently told us, "Those from the West often say they come to empower us as if they are the ones dispensing power. We don't need you to empower us; we need you to simply accompany us in the work we are already doing."

Here's the bottom line: we can't contend until we have spent significant time immersing ourselves in the role of learners rather than heroes. Immersion requires us to linger, be present day in and day out, and listen longer than feels comfortable. Immersion requires that we intentionally displace ourselves so we have the eyes to see the people and places we have been taught not to see.

We often overlook the fact that Jesus spent the vast majority of his life living a mundane and everyday reality among his Galilean community. Jesus didn't arrive on the scene of humanity's brokenness, run out of an ambulance, and start resuscitating us. Instead, he made himself one with the humanity he came to redeem. He made himself vulnerable and reliant on the comfort and care of the broken. He studied in our schools, sat around our tables, had dirt under his fingernails and the smell of fish on his hands. In a slow, all-of-life commitment, Jesus made our reality his reality. God intentionally displaced himself in Jesus so that he could accompany us to restoration.

ACCOMPANY RATHER THAN EMPOWER

The border between San Diego and Tijuana is the most-crossed international border in the world. In fact, although in two different countries, these two cities depend on one another socially, environmentally, politically, and economically. If you were looking from a satellite, you'd never know they were two cities but assume they were one large metropolitan area.

Tijuana is also the most "evangelized" city in the world. Just to its north there is a church flush with money and plenty of desire to serve. Many of us have participated in short-term mission trips where we held a vacation Bible school or built a house in an under-resourced part of northern Mexico. We both have participated in and led trips like this during our tenures as youth pastors. While many remarkable things happened and some degree of relationship was established as a result of our service, we've rethought this ministry strategy as we've built long-term friendships with church leaders in Tijuana.

A few years ago we sat with our friend Luis, a Mexican pastor in Tijuana who every day gives his life to care for boys who no longer have family to support them. At one point we asked him what he thought about the presence of the North American church in Tijuana and our short-term mission movement.

Luis looked at us with both frustration and grace and said, "Nothing has demobilized the church of Tijuana more than the North American mission movement. You come in for one week a year to build a house or host a vacation Bible school and leave. Do you know how dependent we've become on your services? Do you know how we've allowed your mission strategy to disempower us from being the church in Tijuana *for* Tijuana?"

He went on to say, "We know you have good intentions and we want to partner with your churches, but slow down, be present, build friendship, and in doing so learn what we actually need."

Luis was describing our North American tendency to immerse in the posture of heroes seeking to save rather than learners longing to understand. Whether we're involved in an international context, a neighborhood park, or an interpersonal relationship, we have to learn how to move toward conflict with humility and curiosity. We must expect to learn as much from those we serve as they do from us. Immersion must model a mutual interdependence that leads to genuine relationship. It is only then that we will be able to contend with any kind of significance.

Only when we immerse in this way do we begin to discern between the need for brain surgeries and bandages.

These are the insights we are gifted with when we expose ourselves to minority voices in the majority world. Learning like this
happens only when we intentionally step off the road of comfort,
power, and privilege and step into what is real. If we take seriously
the counsel of those like Luis and Gilberto, we will begin to immerse to the degree that our contending will actually become
constructive. We will no longer be fixing things that aren't broken
or fixing things in all the wrong ways. We will be linking arms
with brothers and sisters across borders and boundaries and
joining them in ushering in the world God is making. We won't
be so driven by the next cause that we trample on the very people
we are called to be in relationship with and serve alongside.

Immersion invites us to slow down and pursue relationship
rather than a quick fix. It is there that we are reminded of our
shared beauty and brokenness. We are all created in the image of
God as equals, and we have all been found by a God who immersed into our broken story in Jesus. When we immerse, we
create space for the Spirit to work in places of brokenness within
ourselves and in others.

A MODEL AND MANDATE TO
MOVE TOWARD CONFLICT

Jesus presents the Samaritan as the one person in the story who
chose to see the way God sees. While the religious elite noticed
the man on the road and walked by, the Samaritan saw the
humanity, dignity, and image of God in the man. As a result, he
was moved to compassion, which fueled responsibility. As we
return to Luke 10, we find four verbs describing the Samaritan's
response that embody *immerse*, our second everyday peacemaking practice.

First, Jesus says the Samaritan "came near him" (Luke 10:33
NRSV). While in the preceding text the religious elite moved

away from the victim, the Samaritan made an intentional choice to move toward him. He had every reason to ignore the man or come up with excuses for why it wasn't his responsibility to engage, but instead he met the man in the midst of his pain, brokenness, and vulnerability.

On the beautiful and broken paths of life, we will inevitably come upon pain and conflict. In that moment we are faced with the decision to ignore the pain or immerse into the center of it. We can act like the dying man doesn't exist, we can convince ourselves he is not our responsibility, or we can make the intentional choice to move deeper into his broken story seeking to understand rather than be understood.

For most of us, the conflict probably won't take the form of a man physically dying on the side of the road.

It will be the relationship with your best friend that fractures and everything in you telling you to ignore the conflict and embrace shallowness and the status quo.

It will be the coworker who doesn't stand up for you when your boss is in the room, sowing seeds of resentment that begin to grow.

It will be the time your spouse breaks your trust, causing you to choose indefinite distance rather than move toward healing and intimacy.

It will be choosing to ignore the neighbor who is isolated, alone, and in desperate need of friendship—or immerse into the situation.

It will be the moment you are confronted by the broken systems that are breaking people in your city or nation.

In all of these we have to ask the question, "Am I going to make the intentional choice to immerse into conflict or ignore it and walk away?"

When the Samaritan chose to come near the voiceless victim, we can imagine he knew he was walking into uncertainty, potential inconvenience, and possible pain. Immersion comes at a cost, but the path of discipleship never promised convenience.

Jesus then says the Samaritan "saw him" (Luke 10:33). As we discussed in the previous chapter, seeing is very different from noticing. In fact, we would argue that because we have been taught to see certain realities and not see others, seeing the way Jesus sees is an intentional act. To illustrate, imagine that we are standing on the beach overlooking the ocean all the way to the horizon. We see a massive blanket of blue water extending as far as the eye can see. It is beautiful in its own right, but it doesn't give us a full picture of the reality in front of us. When we put on our wetsuit and scuba gear and immerse into the water, we encounter a whole new reality. We see a canvas of color, life, and texture. We see reality.

Immersion requires us to step off the road of comfort, complacency, and misunderstanding and step into the beauty and brokenness of reality.

We can often be deceived into thinking we know people based on skin color, economic standing, accent, faith tradition, or social location. The reality is that we rarely know anything based on these factors. We have to move beyond our knee-jerk assumptions and learn to truly see those who look, think, act, or believe differently than we do.

The Samaritan then was "moved with pity" (Luke 10:33 NRSV). More than sadness, pity is a sense of compassion that fuels merciful action. This level of compassion doesn't come from hearing someone's story of pain or conflict; it comes from experiencing it ourselves. The Samaritan had immersed so deeply into this man's broken story that the man's pain became the Samaritan's pain. When we immerse to this degree, our compassion fuels responsibility and leads to action. The Samaritan could no longer walk away and neither can we.

Immersion taps into our most sacred human desire and calling to love. When an injustice or conflict becomes more than theoretical, affecting a real person, our world is turned upside down and there is no way to return to the path we once walked. When we immerse, we become free to experience the intimacy and interdependence of our shared humanity.

Finally, Luke 10:33 says, "He went to him." Knowing the extent of this man's situation, the Samaritan chose to immerse no matter what it would cost him in time, money, reputation, or safety. He had been invited into a whole new reality and he couldn't imagine a scenario where he wasn't a key player of redemption within it. To walk away from the dying man was to walk away from the opportunity to join in God's mission of reconciliation.

While the actions of the Samaritan help us understand what immersion can look like, we also have to identify the obstacles that will stand in our way if we take this way of life seriously.

OBSTACLES TO IMMERSION

As we've been discussing throughout this chapter, immersion requires an intentional movement toward conflict. It is challenging, it takes guts, and there is no way to know how things will work out in the end. Immersion forces us to consider the cost and implications of saying "yes" to our vocation as everyday peacemakers. As we've lived this out over the years in our local contexts and walked with others doing the same domestically and internationally, we've come to recognize three primary obstacles to immersion.

Busyness and overcommitment. Because our Western culture places such a high value on production and accomplishment of tasks, we are running ourselves into the ground with busyness. We become such slaves to our calendars that often when we are asked, "How are you doing?" we respond, "Busy." We aren't pointing fingers here—we continually have to examine this tendency in our own lives. We are both married, have young kids, are engaged in our neighborhoods and faith communities, and try to make space for fun, travel, personal development, and sleep. It's exhausting just typing that out, let alone living it.

Many if not most of you can relate to this reality and are probably beginning to feel a healthy tension as you read about stepping into a life and practice of peacemaking. You may be asking how you can possibly make room for another commitment in your already overcommitted life.

We aren't advising that you add anything. Instead, we suggest that you evaluate what could be removed from or adjusted in your schedule to create the necessary margin to be present to the voiceless victim in your own context. What would happen if we simply lifted our eyes from our screens and looked into the eyes of our neighbors?

My (Jon's) family recently moved three doors down on the same street where we've lived for years. We were shocked by how this seemingly insignificant move affected the dynamics of our daily life with neighbors. The neighbor we used to say hello to over a cup of coffee each morning was replaced with someone far too busy to pause for that interaction. Our other direct neighbors, with whom we shared a fruit tree, were replaced by someone who would rather cut the tree down than share in its produce. We found that although all our neighbors were still in the same places, our day-to-day interactions were shifting, and we had to create space in our schedule to be present to them.

So we carved out time in the late afternoon to linger on our front patio with our kiddos riding their scooters, eating dirt, and connecting with neighbors as they came home from work. Because it's physically impossible not to see our family (we have four young kids), most of our new neighbors ended up saying hello or hanging out on the patio with us within the first couple of months of living in our new place. We are becoming characters in the story of our neighborhood in a new way as the Spirit awakens us to new realities and relationships.

It doesn't sound like much, but this small act of descheduling our day took a lot of intentionality. Our lives had become so programmed for busyness and efficiency that we had to step into a countercultural practice of presence to see and immerse into what God had placed right in front of us. Here's the bottom line: immersion is rarely convenient. It usually takes more time than we anticipate. Allowing the Spirit to lead us into a reorientation of time and efficiency helps us overcome the obstacle of busyness.

Image management and our investment in personal reputation. One of the reasons the religious elite hesitated to help the dying man was the possibility of tainting their reputation and compromising their ritual cleanliness. They were to honor God and represent God's people by living as those set apart from the "unclean" people and practices of the world. Interestingly, it is Jesus who upends this narrative by portraying the "unclean" Samaritan as the model of service, faithfulness, and "cleanliness," not the "clean" religious elite.

Our Christian culture often takes a similar posture toward "the other" (whoever that may be in our context) today. We often fall victim to viewing our faith as something we must preserve, guard, and defend. As such, we think that if we move toward relationships with those we differ from or disagree with, we will somehow compromise the integrity of our faith. If we associate with the wrong people in the wrong places, we may fall down the slippery slope of compromise. As we've stated earlier, moving toward the other doesn't compromise our faith; it reflects the very best of it. In fact, it is when we move toward the other that we act as Jesus did and embrace our vocation as everyday peacemakers.

One of the most significant obstacles to moving toward the other is the fear of compromising our image and personal reputation. When we say "yes" to Jesus' call to immerse into the lives and stories of others, it will cost us something, and we will probably be misunderstood, ridiculed, and even hated by friends, family, and colleagues. Brian McLaren argues that we all find ourselves with inherited "us" and "them" spheres that frame our social identity and interactions. Jesus' mandate is to move toward those within the "them" sphere no matter the cost. But in our movement toward "them," those in our "us" sphere will often feel threatened, confused, and protective. When we encounter critique and potential name-calling from those we love most in our lives, our convictions will be tested. Do we continue to move toward "them" in faithfulness or do we retreat back to "us" in order to protect our image and reputation?

In our experience, this is an inevitable reality for the everyday peacemaker who takes seriously the call to immerse into the lives and stories of voiceless victims. This has been one of the biggest challenges we've faced in living this way of life. The more we've built mutually beneficial relationships with friends of different skin tones, nationalities, traditions, and orientations, the more caution flags began to wave among those closest to us. Is he going too far? If he continues to associate with people of different faiths will he lose his own? Is he trying to make a political statement by standing with the undocumented community in his neighborhood? Does he no longer believe in the authority of Scripture because of his deep friendships within the _____ community? At best, these were honest questions. At worst, they were assumptions about the content of our character. In either case they were hard to hear. These kinds of questions call into question our faithfulness, credibility, and reputation. But while we are not actively trying to disappoint those closest to us, their perspective is not the force behind our daily practice as Jesus-following everyday peacemakers.

Fear. Most people avoid conflict because it carries with it too much potential pain and violence. Whether in our interpersonal relationships or an international context, we often think we're better off acting like conflict doesn't exist so we can remain at peace. But this pseudo-peace simply brushes the source of the conflict under the rug for it to later grow into resentment and more devastating violence. Conflict isn't only something to be resolved; it's an opportunity to be transformed.

In order for transformation to occur, we must take that scary first and second and third step toward it. We can't run from it in fear. We must learn to trust the Spirit's leading and expect God's best work to unfold because of our faithfulness to lean in rather than isolate and insulate ourselves.

We live in a culture that's addicted to safety and security. And in light of our global state of violence and instability, we can understand why. Conversations ranging from our coffee shops to the halls of political power are focused on the necessity to pursue security and safety above anything else. As fathers of little kids, we have never experienced a season of life when we'd be more tempted to pursue security and safety above all else. We can't begin to comprehend the disorientation and paralyzing pain that would come with harm to our families.

For the past six years we have been traveling to conflict zones in the Middle East, but the more kids we have waiting for us to return home safely, the more significant the implications for us of stepping on that plane and deciding to move toward potential violence. When we hear our politicians talk about the paramount importance of "security" and "safety," it strikes a chord, and we could find ourselves tempted to blindly agree.

Interestingly, the more we follow Jesus, the more our allegiance to safety begins to dissipate. Our wives often tell us as we leave, "I'll pray for your safety, but more, I'll pray that you follow Jesus toward the people and places you are called to be among." Our kingdom allegiance is marked by one who moved toward rather than away from potential violence. We're convinced that our desire to affirm this "security at any cost" rhetoric is a temptation to worship the idol of safety. It is not something to be admired; it is something to be acknowledged, questioned, and repented of (turned away from).

A faith that worships the idol of safety will pray for our undocumented friends without standing with them in the face of family separation via deportation.

A faith that worships the idol of safety will offer premature diagnoses to people's problems on the other side of the world without ever having immersed into their reality.

A faith that worships the idol of safety will critique people of color in their pain rather than participate in their restoration.

Worshiping the idol of safety greatly inhibits our ability to worship the crucified and risen Jesus by immersing ourselves into the center of the story we've been called to tell with our lives.

When we worship the idol of safety, we can quickly compromise our kingdom witness and begin to justify the means through which safety is achieved. For example, when we celebrate the death of other human beings because it means we are "safer," we may be worshiping the idol of safety rather than the enemy-loving God embodied in Jesus. When we demonize and punish entire groups of people (the vast majority of whom have no desire to do us harm) for the sake of our "safety," we may be worshiping the idol of safety rather than a Jesus who loved indiscriminately. When we reject the very people who are fleeing violence (many of whom are children) for the sake of our "safety," we may be worshiping the idol of safety rather than a Jesus who calls us to care for the strangers in our midst. Finally, while these may feel like safety measures, it is increasingly clear that these means don't lead to a lasting, sustainable security. They more often lead to resentment, oppression, and instability, which breeds more violence.

As we've wrestled with this idol of safety, we've repeatedly been convicted by this truth: Jesus never called us to be safe. He called us to be faithful. According to Jesus, faithfulness moves us beyond love of neighbor to love of enemy. If pursuit of our safety trumps our ability to love whoever God has in our path, fear wins and we distance ourselves from God's heart for the world. How can we love our "enemy" if we don't know them? The idol of safety moves us away from people who are different from us and sends us inward to those who look, think, and act like we do. There is no love outside of relationship; there is only misunderstanding, demonization, and stereotype. How can we know our "enemy" if we don't cross the borders that divide us? The Jesus way requires us to reject the temptation to move inward and continually calls us to move toward the other.

Jesus models to the world life as it was meant to be lived. His is a life marked not by isolation or triumphant overthrow but by suffering, sacrifice, and selfless love for the flourishing of others. It is a life that crosses borders and boundaries to reassign the humanity, dignity, and image of God in all the "wrong" people—those he should have feared and stayed away from. A life that ended with the uttering of this prayer for his enemies: "Father, forgive them, for they do not know what they are doing" (Luke 23:34).

Imagine if instead Jesus chose to worship the idol of safety and never left the security of his little Galilean synagogue so he could read Torah and remain isolated from the violence of the world?

Let's pay attention to our understandable levels of fear, paralysis, and temptation to worship the idol of safety rather than take the next faithful step. This is not easy stuff, but friends, this is the beauty, challenge, and mystery of choosing to follow an enemy-loving God. He invites us to love to the point of death with the hope and reality of resurrection as our fuel.

WHEN THE STUDENT BECOMES THE TEACHER AND EVERYTHING CHANGES

We recently hosted a group of academics on the United States-Mexico border as part of our Immigrants' Journey Immersion Trips, which represented nearly a half-million college students from Christian universities and colleges around the country. After two unforgettable days touring the border wall with patrol agents, hearing the stories of leading immigration activists, and sharing meals with recently deported men in Tijuana, the trip ended with an encounter that rattled us to our core.

We heard the story of Juanita, a twenty-two-year-old un-documented woman who was brought into the United States by her parents when she was a baby. Because her experience as an undocumented person living in the United States is in-credibly common (there are currently 12 million undocumented people in the United States) yet also misunderstood, we asked, "What is it like to live in the shadows day in and day out as an undocumented person?"

Juanita spoke with strength and prophetic conviction in front of a group that would have intimidated most fifty-year-old women, let alone a twenty-two-year-old. She shared about her passion for photography, which led to her being accepted into one of the most prestigious art schools in the country when she was eighteen. It was at this point that her parents re-vealed—to her shock—Juanita's undocumented status, which forced her to turn down the life-changing offer. She was crushed and hope was lost.

What other vocational roadblocks would she run into because of her status? Was she safe telling her closest friends, or could that lead to her deportation? How was she supposed to process the reality that, through no fault of her own, she must turn away from the path of prestige and reputation in order to hide from prestige and reputation?

Despite her disappointment, Juanita refused to become apathetic. Instead she channeled her frustration toward creating opportunities for younger kids in her situation to find a path toward citizenship. She mentored, coached, led workshops, and advocated on their behalf as a way to use her story and experience redemptively. By immersing themselves into Juanita's story, each president, provost, and professor sitting in that room confronted the fact that Juanita wasn't a leach on our society but a core contributor to what's best about our society.

When she was done sharing, there was a heavy silence that descended on the group as they took in what they had heard. After a few seconds, one of the participants leaned in, looked Juanita in the eye, and said, "We would be honored to have you at our university and want to offer you a full-ride scholarship to do so."

It was a moment when heaven crashed into earth as each participant was confronted with a reality they had previously been blind to. They had to be immersed into a story far outside their everyday reality for them to see the way Jesus sees. They had to adopt the posture of a learner rather than a hero to see the humanity, dignity, and image of God in Juanita.

Juanita is a perfect example of someone we have been taught not to see. Our neighbors without documents are often referred to as "illegals" or "aliens," which robs them of their unique personhood and shared humanity. Culturally, whether directly or indirectly, we are taught that "they" are problems to fix rather than mothers, fathers, sisters, brothers, and friends worthy of our love, compassion, and care. And, we would argue, they often have more to teach us about generosity, hard work, and family values than we do them. When we immerse into the story of the other by stepping off the road of comfort and into reality, we are given the gift of seeing a full range of beauty, color, and complexity inherent in humanity.

We are all invited to immerse into the center of conflict by stepping off the beaten path of comfort and complacency in the posture of a learner rather than a hero.

PRACTICAL STRATEGIES FOR IMMERSION

It's important for us to take tangible steps to move from theory to embodied everyday practices. Here are a few suggestions; we encourage you to discern which one resonates with you and to take one step to live it out this week.

Learn another language. Choose one that is common in your neighborhood or workplace. Shaun and Maria are on our Global Immersion team and are deeply embedded in their neighborhood near the border. In addition to teaching English classes at their neighborhood community center, they pair English speakers with Spanish speakers in their community with the goal of each learning a desired second language. These pairings have the added benefit of cultivating friendships among people from different cultures who would not otherwise have any connection. This is a mutual way to move toward one another in a spirit of curiosity. The doors it will open for everyday peacemaking will be countless.

Sit on your front patio rather than in your backyard. This is a decision both of our families made years ago. It's incredible how we are invited into the life of our neighborhood by being visible and accessible to our neighbors and those walking our streets.

Further, it's countercultural—many people are so surprised that they can't help but say hello.

Identify the "other" in your community. We are in a time in history where we don't have to travel across the world to be in relationship with people from all over it. Identify your local refugee resettlement agency and host a family in their transition to your city. Bring your kids with you!

Invite a neighbor into your home for a meal or join a local community sports league. Pay attention to the ways you can invite others toward you and say "yes" to invitations from others. Jesus made himself fully vulnerable to humanity; what might that vulnerability look like for you in your neighborhood?

Consider enrolling your kids in your neighborhood school. This is often where the rubber meets the road in a sometimes costly way. What if your primary deciding factors weren't about what you or your kids could receive from the school but what you could bring to it? You certainly will receive many blessings, but they may not look like what you first imagined.

Spend time at a coffee shop or pub in a neighborhood you wouldn't normally visit. Pay attention to the different faces and realities that exist there that you may not have had eyes to see otherwise. What are you observing and learning about what is real in that community?

REFLECT AND DISCUSS

1. Have you ever intentionally stepped off the road of comfort and into the reality of conflict? If not, why not? If so, what was it like?

2. What obstacle limits you from immersing yourself deeper into the broken systems and broken lives around you?

3. What does Jesus' immersion into our human neighborhood as a vulnerable, poor refugee child tell us about what our posture should be?

4. Have you become a slave to maintaining your image and reputation among your friends, family, and community? What spiritual practices do you need to put into place to understand that your identity isn't based on the affirmation of the "us" but faithfulness to immerse into the lives and stories of "them"?

5. What are two or three practices that will help you immerse deeper into your own neighborhood and into the realities of others?

SEVEN

CONTEND

One of our mentors in the practices of peace is a Mexican man named Oscar. Roughly thirty years ago, he was asked to start a YMCA program that would serve Tijuana. As a result, Oscar and his family found themselves in a new city, and they began to listen to stories and keep their eyes open to how God might be moving. The longer they were in the city, the more they began to see an injustice that left them no choice other than immersion.

What Oscar saw was plenty of arms waiting to welcome young children who had just been deported to Tijuana—many of which represented the embrace of organized crime. The children, terrified and desperate for any form of care and support, rushed into those arms. And then these "caretakers" turned around and sold the children into sex slavery, forced labor, and other insidious evils. The deeper Oscar immersed into their story, the clearer it became that he was being called to contend for the flourishing of these children.

It began with a boy named Enrique.

Enrique was deported into the streets and sewers of Tijuana and began associating with a group of kids with a similar story. As is the case with most who have been deported, Enrique made it his mission to get back into the United States where his family, friends, and therefore his future existed. Without support, most deportees end up destitute within five days.

One day, while trying to cross back into the United States, he was shot in the back by an FBI agent. He fell to the ground as the bullet lodged itself in his spine, paralyzing him from the waist down.

Not only had Enrique failed to get back to his family, he was now cast back into the streets of Tijuana in a wheelchair with no support or hope for a better future. It was in this season that Oscar first encountered Enrique. Because he had no other options, the dreamer-turned-parapalegic was working as a pawn in the system of organized crime.

When Oscar met Enrique, now a teenager, his feet dangled on the ground because the legs of his wheelchair had broken off. His feet were mangled and infected, yet he had no choice but to continue on for the sake of survival. Oscar immersed into this dark, painful story with compassion, offering simply to clean Enrique's damaged feet.

As their relationship deepened, seeds of trust began to grow. Oscar invited this physically broken, emotionally damaged pawn of organized crime into his home (with his wife and children) in order to bandage his feet on a regular basis. They invited Enrique to their table for warm, nutritious meals and eventually asked him to live with them.

Soon Enrique no longer identified himself as deported, physically broken, and emotionally damaged. He was able to see himself as what he had been all along: a sacred creation made in the image of God with a hope for a future of flourishing.

The road was long, costly, and at times downright ugly, but once Oscar and his family saw Enrique and immersed into his story, they had no choice but to contend for his restoration. Their contending didn't stop with bandaging feet but involved long-term emotional and psychological healing.

Everyday peacemakers must be careful not to assume they know what the practice of contending should look like until they have immersed themselves deep into the story of the broken, seeking to understand rather than to be understood. In other words, quick fixes based on what we perceive initially may not actually be helpful in the long term. Immersion helps us to contend intelligently and compassionately.

Oscar is always quick to point out that we can't control how the story ends, but we can surely be faithful in the midst of it. Oscar was faithful, modeling the gritty, subversive, and costly work of peacemaking.

A THEOLOGY OF CONTENDING

Let's return to Jesus' story of the Good Samaritan in which the lowly, despised, half-breed upended the status quo. While the religious elite failed to see the image of God in the plight of the voiceless victim on the side of the road, the Samaritan exemplified the practice of seeing by willingly encountering the man's humanity. The religious, concerned with their reputation and ritual purity, chose avoidance rather than immersion, while the Samaritan, moved to compassion, had no choice but to immerse into the center of the man's broken reality.

Then, to the surprise of all who listened to this parable, Jesus raised up the Samaritan as the embodiment of contending. It was the Samaritan who rolled up his sleeves to work for the flourishing of the exploited, voiceless victim in tangible, costly ways.

First, the Samaritan bandaged the man's wounds. In other words, he got down on the victim's level and got his hands dirty. There is nothing pretty about cleaning and bandaging open wounds. This probably forced the man to endure excruciating pain and made him completely vulnerable to the Samaritan. We learn that contending doesn't happen from a distance but through standing in the midst of the brokenness together. Our proximity to the "other" shapes our ability to contend in costly and creative ways.

Second, the Samaritan poured oil and wine on the wounds. In context this would have represented an "anointing" of the man, not only to initiate the physical healing process but to reassign him his dignity as a human being. We discover that contending leads us to humanize those we often view as less than human.

Third, the Samaritan loaded the man on his mule. This action shows the inconvenience and cost of contending. Not only did the Samaritan give up his seat; he physically lifted the victim up, putting the weight of injustice on himself. Contending requires that we put the flourishing of others ahead of our personal comfort and convenience.

Fourth, the Samaritan brought the man to an inn—and took care of him. The journey on the Jericho road is long and treacherous, and no doubt the Samaritan was ready to get on with his business and be done with this goodwill "project." But neither the danger nor the demands of his schedule caused the Samaritan to walk away. He not only brought the man to the safety of the inn but stuck around and took care of him. Contending requires personal resolve and long-term commitment.

Fifth, the Samaritan financed the man's healing. The text says the Samaritan gave the innkeeper two days' wages to cover the man's stay. Scholars argue that two days' wages would have allowed the man to stay in the inn with supervised care for two weeks to two months. Rather than short-term benevolence, the man receives nearly a monthlong residence that would allow him to get back on his feet. We learn that contending is expensive and requires each of us to confront how we steward our resources. *Lastly, the Samaritan involved others in the man's restoration.* Knowing it wasn't sustainable to contend on his own, the Samaritan asked the innkeeper to look after the man until he returned. Often we feel as though the weight of the world were on our individual shoulders and when we try to bear the weight, it crushes us and renders us useless for the long haul. We have to involve others if we are to contend successfully in the long term.

In this story Jesus offers us a compelling and provocative picture of what contending for the flourishing of others looks like. It's not an intellectual ideal, a Facebook campaign, or a vote for your favorite politician—contending is costly and tangible. It requires creativity in the midst of brokenness. It may require compromising some of our religious ideals or reputation for the sake of others. It requires that we offer our precious time when we have plenty of other things vying for it. It may require that we open our wallets and choose to live on less so that others can get on their feet. And for contending to be sustainable, it most certainly requires community. As with other elements of discipleship, we were not created to walk this path alone.

We have regularly, throughout history, skipped the practices of seeing and immersing ourselves and jumped straight to contending. Because we like to fix things as quickly as possible and move on to the next thing, we have often failed to sit in the brokenness long enough to discern what contending should look like. In doing so, we either offer a short-term bandage solution or actually cause more harm than good by acting on an incorrect understanding of what helping should entail.

Like the Samaritan, we must be people who first see like Jesus sees and immerse into the brokenness or conflict seeking to understand rather than be understood. Only then will we discern what contending will require of us. In the end we may confront some brokenness in ourselves and find that we are the ones most in need of healing.

JESUS' TEACHING AND LIFE AS A MODEL OF CONTENDING

Contending for justice and working for the healing of broken things is central to the story of God and the work of his people. Whether it's broken people or the systems that break them, God is consistently moving to the center of these conflicts with the heart and actions of the Healer.

Even when God seemed absent during dark seasons of exile, God whispered through the voices of the Hebrew prophets that one was coming who would bring justice by waging a decisive peace.

> For to us a child is born,
>> to us a son is given,
>> and the government will be on his shoulders.
> And he will be called
>> Wonderful Counselor, Mighty God,
>> Everlasting Father, Prince of Peace. (Isaiah 9:6)

> Rejoice greatly, Daughter Zion!
>> Shout, Daughter Jerusalem!
> See, your king comes to you,
>> righteous and victorious,
> lowly and riding on a donkey,
>> on a colt, the foal of a donkey. (Zechariah 9:9)

Throughout the biblical text, the word for "justice" is used more than a thousand times. While some use the terms interchangeably, we think it's important to distinguish between justice-seeking and peacemaking. Throughout Scripture God always placed himself on the side of justice and called his people to do the same. Inherent in human society are personal and systemic injustices that tilt the scales of equality and equity away from those without power. To pursue justice requires exposing the imbalance and reforming systems and structures such that all are free to flourish. Author and activist Cornel West says, "Never forget that justice is what love looks like in public." Justice is the hard work of reordering broken systems and individual patterns that don't look like love.

Our friend Mae Cannon, author of *Social Justice Handbook*, writes, "If God commanded all people to be stewards of the earth, we can assume he desires all people to have access to the earth's resources. When access to those resources is unequally distributed or abused by those in power, social justice is impeded." David Gushee and the late Glen Stassen have done extensive work drawing parallels between the prophet Isaiah's themes for justice and the justice proposed by and embodied in Jesus. According to their study, the four themes of justice that move through the Old Testament and into the New Testament with Jesus involve an end to (1) unjust economic structures, (2) unjust domination, (3) unjust violence, and (4) unjust exclusion from community.

These themes culminate in Jesus' sermon in Nazareth when he quotes the prophet Isaiah in Luke 4:16-19:

> He went to Nazareth, where he had been brought up, and on the Sabbath day he went into the synagogue, as was his custom. He stood up to read, and the scroll of the prophet Isaiah was handed to him. Unrolling it, he found the place where it is written:

"The Spirit of the Lord is on me,
    because he has anointed me
    to proclaim good news to the poor.
He has sent me to proclaim freedom for the prisoners
    and recovery of sight for the blind,
    to set the oppressed free,
    to proclaim the year of the Lord's favor."

Justice-seeking is something all Christians are called to do and a key component of peacemaking, but the two aren't synonymous. Peacemaking is a formational journey of discipleship with a tangible set of practices that are continually adjusting our posture according to the cross and aligning us with the mission of God. Peacemaking is the journey to a holistic salvation or shalom. There is no path to this holistic shalom outside of justice. Peacemakers who see and immerse will inherently encounter injustice and be called to join God in righting wrongs.

In short, peacemaking is the journey and justice is one of the central components of walking the journey with integrity. Our third everyday peacemaking practice, contend, is where our call to justice is fleshed out in tangible, costly, and creative ways. Through Jesus' words and embodied in his life, we get a robust understanding of what contending is in everyday life.

In the Sermon on the Mount, Jesus offers a manifesto for what life looks like for the people of God. While he addresses numerous topics on life and faith, in Matthew 5:38-42 he gives specific insight into how the Jesus community is to deal with conflict and violence at the hand of an oppressor:

"You have heard that it was said, 'Eye for eye, and tooth for tooth.' But I tell you, do not resist an evil person. If anyone slaps you on the right cheek, turn to them the other cheek also. And if anyone wants to sue you and take your shirt, hand over your coat as well. If anyone forces you to go one mile, go with them two miles. Give to the one who asks you, and do not turn away from the one who wants to borrow from you."

Jesus' words in this passage could be summarized like this: "We aren't to face violence and helplessly be run over by it, nor are we to fight violence with more violence." Many scholars have offered commentaries on the significance of these passages in the context of first-century Roman occupation, and most agree that Jesus is proposing something very different from a passive response to violence. We aren't to face violence and helplessly get run over by it. Rather, we are to confront violence with creativity such that our dignity is magnified and the evil of the oppressor is exposed. In short, there is a third way—a way that neither plays by the rules of violent revenge nor passively withdraws from conflict in fear.

After Jesus spent his life teaching his followers what it meant to contend, he made his most powerful point through his actions. In Luke 19 we find Jesus making his way toward Jerusalem. Many expected this Messiah to contend for and restore the people of God through military conquest and overthrow of their oppressors. But as we know, that's not how the story goes.

Jesus, while looking out over Jerusalem, began to weep. He did not weep because there was conflict; he wept because of how his people were engaging it. Rather than living out the teachings from the Sermon on the Mount he so eloquently proclaimed on the hills of Galilee, they continued to sow seeds of violence and maintain an expectation that Jesus would do the same.

It is from here that Jesus lived out the message he had been communicating all along. We witness a Messiah who didn't take back the throne through military might but through selfless suffering and sacrifice. Jesus contended for our flourishing by absorbing our brokenness so we could find healing. We see that on the cross, the most decisive act of contending didn't lead to fighting and violence but giving oneself as a recipient of violence for the flourishing of all.

TRANSFORMING INITIATIVES

The late Glen Stassen was our friend and mentor in peacemaking and reconciliation. Arguably, his most lasting contribution that will shape his legacy was his development of the "just peace-making" theory, an alternative to the just war theory and to pacifism. After decades as a scholar and practitioner, Stassen built this paradigm based on Jesus' teachings in the Sermon on the Mount and grounded in the reality of global conflict.

Stassen articulated both the value and shortcomings of traditional interpretations of just war and pacifism. While there is significant nuance to both models that we won't get into here, it is important to briefly unpack each of their core components.

The just war theory was developed by Augustine of Hippo in the fourth century after Christianity became the religion of the Roman Empire. Jesus-followers were trying to figure out how to retain Christian witness in a world where enemies sought to acquire land and power through violent attack. Just war theory became a framework used to justify killing in war as long as the reasons for doing so were important enough to override the truth that killing fellow human beings is wrong.

Just war theory relies on eight criteria to determine whether a violent response to injustice (war) is justified. These criteria are used as a way to govern against rash decisions and violent responses and to reduce the amount of violence. Historically, the church has widely accepted this ethic for war and peace, but we have also misused it to justify violence in the name of imperial conquest, ascribing God's blessing to the church's bloody endeavors.

Pacifism predates the just war theory in that the early church almost unanimously practiced nonviolence for the first three hundred years of its existence. After an exhaustive study of early Christianity, Ron Sider concluded that violence is never an option for the Christ follower. This conviction lies at the heart of Christian expressions like the Anabaptists, Quakers, Franciscans, Brethren, and many others.

While theologians and leaders such as John Howard Yoder, Dietrich Bonheoffer, and Martin Luther King Jr. have identified dozens of varieties of pacifism, the core value is a strict adherence to the nonviolence of Jesus and an unwillingness to compromise Christian witness if violence is used. At its worst, pacifism (in practice) can be mistaken with passivism, a withdrawal or removal from conflict—a disengagement. When pacifism takes this distorted form, it renders itself complicit with violence and injustice in its absence from it.

Stassen argues that just war theory is valuable in that it calls for active engagement in conflict for the sake of standing with those on the underside of violence. His critique of just war is that it justifies moving toward violence with violence. On the other hand, Stassen affirms pacifism in its commitment to nonviolence and belief that violence doesn't bring an end to violence but simply perpetuates it. His critique—and again this isn't true in all pacifist traditions—is that pacifists often withdraw from conflict altogether, which makes them complicit in the continued violence and domination of the abused.

Not only because of his dissatisfaction with these two approaches to conflict but drawing on the mandate in Jesus' words and deeds, Stassen argues for just peacemaking as a third way. Just peacemaking highlights the value of both traditions while maintaining faithfulness to the Jesus way. Like the just war theory, just peacemaking requires that we move directly toward conflict on behalf of the abused. But rather than entering conflict with the weapons of war, we enter with weapons that make for peace. It is here that he affirms the pacifist tradition of nonviolence.

Echoing John Paul Lederach's theory of conflict transformation, Stassen would argue that conflict isn't inherently a bad thing; it's just that we have no idea how to engage it constructively. When we are armed with the weapons of transformation, conflict is the seedbed for healing and can deepen genuine relationship. So what are these weapons of transformation?

What we call the practice of contending Stassen calls "transforming initiatives." In the same way that Jesus calls us to respond to violence with creative alternatives that disarm the abuser and reassign dignity to the abused (see Matthew 5:38-42), we must develop a set of practices that embody this third approach to conflict. In other words, rather than getting even and perpetuating the violence, we must learn to get creative in love.

Like Jesus' call to walk the extra mile, turn the other cheek, and hand over our coat, transforming initiatives are contending practices that allow us to move to the center of conflict transformatively. These are the practices that mobilize us as peacemakers in the gritty realities of everyday life.

EMBODYING THE UNORTHODOX
INVITATION TO CREATIVE LOVE

Recently, a street preacher on the steps of a Christian university, Bible in hand, was yelling some remarkably hateful things at students as they walked by. While the preacher may have considered his words an act of contending for the students, the content of his speech ran in sharp contrast to the teachings of Jesus, and the manner in which he chose to communicate equally contradicted the life Jesus lived.

If they were to contend not by getting even but getting creative in love, what responses could the students initiate? Should they align with just war theory and get in this guy's face and say equally hateful things back to him? Maybe physically harm or remove him? Aligning with some in the pacifist tradition, should they simply remove themselves from the situation and walk away, allowing this man to continue his hateful rant at the expense of others?

Rather than options one or two, these students chose a third way: they got creative in love.

In this incredibly intense moment, one of the students put his guitar over his shoulder and softly began singing, "How He Loves Us." As his voice grew louder and more confident, students started trickling toward him and formed a circle around the street preacher. In unison their voices began to rise together in this beautiful song about the endless love of God for his people.

"He loves us; oh, how he loves us; oh, how he loves us; oh, how he loves . . ."

Soon their voices overtook the shouting of the man and he was completely disarmed. He shrugged and gave up.

No stones were thrown.

No hateful words were returned.

No relationships were divided.

The abuser was exposed.

Dignity was restored.

And although they certainly could have, the students didn't ignore the conflict and run away.

DOES JESUS ENDORSE VIOLENCE?

We can't with integrity talk about Jesus' mandate toward peace and nonviolence without acknowledging two difficult passages often used to portray Jesus as one who condones violence:

"Do not suppose that I have come to bring peace to the earth. I did not come to bring peace, but a sword." (Matthew 10:34)

He said to them, "But now if you have a purse, take it, and also a bag; and if you don't have a sword, sell your cloak and buy one." (Luke 22:36)

Biblical scholars have done extensive work to unpack these passages in the context of the original language, the sociopolitical reality of the first century under Roman occupation, the life and teachings of Jesus, and the larger narrative of the Gospels in relation to violence. With that in mind, there are two elements we want to highlight for the sake of this conversation.

First, neither of these passages endorses violence. Rather, they are warnings of coming persecution and division for those who pursue the kingdom of God over and above the empire of Rome. The Matthew passage is set in the context of Jesus' redefinition of family in light of the kingdom. Family is no longer constrained to bloodline but applies to all of humanity. As such, Jesus' followers must be prepared for resistance, division, and even persecution for expanding their definition of who is worthy of their love and affection. The "sword" is a metaphor for the way Jesus' invitation will inevitably disrupt culture, tradition, and religion.

The Luke passage is sandwiched between examples of the high cost of the Jesus way—it comes right after Jesus' prediction of Peter's denial and right before his pleading with God in the garden of Gethsemane to keep him from his pending crucifixion. The disciples missed the point by saying they already had two swords. We can imagine Jesus rolling his eyes and saying, "Enough with your expectation of violence!"

Later in Gethsemane, one of the disciples actually uses the sword and draws blood of the "enemy" (Luke 22:49-51). Jesus quickly reminds him that using the sword only contributes to the cycle of violence and retaliation. It wouldn't be long after Jesus' death and resurrection that his predictions of persecution would come true under Roman tyrants. By that point, his followers understood Jesus' mandate of nonviolence and remained true to it despite the costs.

Second, we can't read these two passages in isolation. When we read the entirety of the Gospels and the New Testament as a whole, the authors are unanimous in their articulation of a Jesus who invites his followers into lives of suffering and self-sacrifice— and who embodied that life himself. While the first-century messianic expectations placed on Jesus would have been of power, military conquest, and violent overthrow, Jesus over and over taught and modeled an alternative way of nonviolence and enemy love. This is how the kingdom came and how we are to participate in its continual manifestation today.

CONTENDING PRACTICES

The reason we don't give a list of contending practices at this point is that they will be unique to every situation, conflict, or reality of brokenness. We can't make them for you, but we can invite you to begin to take Jesus' words seriously and attempt to live in such a way that they are true.

In other words, contending practices come about through the work of the Holy Spirit after we learn to see and immerse. Because everyday peacemaking is an act of discipleship, we are constantly "in process." We have to train every day in this costly, redemptive work so that when these moments arise, our first response isn't getting even but getting creative in love. It is slow and hard and beautiful and different every time.

So how do you contend when you are spiraling deeper into that argument with your spouse? When you are encountering systemic injustice in your neighborhood? How do you contend when your family reunion takes a quick turn for the worse? When a trusted friend or neighbor violates that trust? When you see the vulnerable being exploited on the streets of your city?

Again, this everyday peacemaking practice of contending is not something that forms in us overnight but that we commit to live into for the long haul. In the same way God has contended for humanity from the first of our many dark hours and continued to do to the point of death on a cross, we are called to contend for others.

Everyday peacemakers move beyond cycles of the status quo and violence in order to seek the flourishing of others through creative, costly initiatives. Everyday peacemakers contend in a way that we stand together in front of any bulldozer that flattens people.

GAIL

Reflecting on the words, life, and practice of peacemaking giants like Dorothy Day, Martin Luther King Jr., or Gandhi makes it easy to think contending is something that happens only on a large scale. This mentality can paralyze us from living as everyday peacemakers in the local spaces where we live, work, and play.

My (Jon's) neighborhood just outside of downtown San Diego is nothing glamorous, but it's full of real people with real issues living real life. Further, my family and I are part of a faith community that is committed to living in the same neighborhood while sharing common rhythms of life, worship, mission, and raising kids. It has been a gift, creating a dynamic (although challenging!) environment in which to live out the practices of everyday peacemaking.

A few years ago, a number of people in our community decided to turn a dusty old plot of dirt wedged between an apartment and an adjacent house into a community garden. Their vision was that it would not only produce food to eat but a way to share life with our neighbors.

One of our neighbors was an older woman frequently seen navigating our streets in her wheelchair, always alone. Our community invited her to join us in transforming the dry dirt into a flourishing garden. As our time with her increased, we found out that she lived in a low-income facility in our neighborhood and was completely estranged from her husband and kids.

Her name was Gail.

We offered her a personal section in the garden, and she began to come to life, lighting up our conversations with her smile and a joy that had been stifled for too long. Our time in the garden was sweet, but we came to find out that true friendship with Gail would cost more than a couple of convenient interactions. Two women in our community, Christiana and Rebecca, suddenly received an emergency call from the hospital in the middle of the night. The doctor said Gail had been rushed in by ambulance and they were the only emergency contacts she could produce.

Over the next few years, contending for Gail looked like washing her clothes, cleaning her apartment, paying her bills, and creating space at our shared table to remind each other of our shared humanity and dignity.

One engaged couple in the community, David and Holly, had planned a very intimate wedding and decided to invite Gail as an honored guest. The day of the wedding, my wife picked Gail up (stuffing her massive wheelchair in our tiny car) and drove out to the majestic rolling hills east of our city. Set in a rustic winery, the wedding took place under a canopy of white lights. As the reception turned to dancing, there was a moment when it was just Gail and me at the table. She offered me her nearly toothless smile, and I could sense she wanted to tell me something. So I leaned over.

"I am so honored to be here," she whispered.

We were no longer Gail's neighbors or friends; we had become her family. The inconvenient, unglamorous, and faithful acts of contending over the long haul reminded Gail of her sacredness and reassigned her the dignity that had escaped her.

About a year later Gail passed away, and our little community hosted a memorial service for her in the garden she helped bring to life. We told stories, laughed, cried, and carved out a little plot that would remain in her honor. In this experience we realized that we hadn't only contended for Gail; she had been contending for us. She gave us the gift of relationship and offered us the opportunity to live fully into who we were created to be: a people who take seriously our call to everyday peacemaking and join God in ushering in the world he is making.

CONTENDING IN BROKEN RELATIONSHIPS AND A BROKEN WORLD

While Gail's story helps give a picture of what contending can look like on a local level, it is important to understand that we are called to contend in *all* areas of conflict.

Contending on an interpersonal level might be as simple as giving your spouse necessary space in the midst of an argument. It might be paying for your child's professional counseling. It might be sitting with a neighbor as they lament the loss of a loved one. It might be giving someone the benefit of the doubt even after they've said or done something hurtful.

As we contend interpersonally, we navigate a fine balance between truth and grace. We don't want to offer so much "grace" that we expose ourselves to abuse, but we also need to find balance between immediately confronting the conflict and allowing the necessary space to constructively come together and move through conflict. We don't want to offer so much time for understanding that we expose ourselves to further abuse, but we also need to stay in the game long enough to explore the potential of reconciliation. That said, there will be times when contending interpersonally needs to involve raw and honest truth-telling. We'd be the first to say that those closest to us have had to contend for us in our brokenness and blindness by saying some really hard stuff. It is in those conversations and interventions that we were able confront our own issues and move toward restoration.

The story of the paralyzed man and his friends in Mark 2 is a beautiful picture of contending on an interpersonal level. Here was a man who should have been cast off and forgotten by society, but instead, his friends saw him, immersed into his broken story, grabbed a corner of his mat, and carried him to the feet of the Healer. Contending in our relationships might mean we grab each other's mats and carry each other to Jesus to find healing and restoration.

Recently we have been invited to contend on an international level with our friend Hector. Hector served in the United States military and spent the vast majority of his life in the United States. That said, Hector wasn't a US citizen and was later permanently deported to Mexico, never to return to his family and the country he loved so much.

Hector now lives in Tijuana and has started a nonprofit to support and mobilize deported veterans of the US military. Each time we guide Immersion Trips into the realties of immigration on the borderlands of San Diego and Tijuana, we sit with Hector and his colleagues to hear their stories and stand with them in their pain. We were introduced to Hector by a local Catholic priest in San Diego named Dermot, a migrant himself who now serves as chaplain to the deported veterans community.

It was in the faithful presence of friends like Dermot and Hector south of the border that we began to learn what it looks like to contend across international borders on behalf of those caught in the wake of broken systems that are breaking people. Dermot saw the humanity, dignity, and image of God in Hector and couldn't walk away. Instead, he immersed into his story and was exposed to an injustice that needed to be interrupted.

In the short term, that interruption may look like Dermot simply remaining in relationship despite borders that divide. In the long term, we pray it leads to wholesale reformation of a broken immigration system in our country and the personal reunification of Hector and his children.

OBSTACLES TO CONTENDING

As we continue to emphasize, peacemaking isn't a soft, euphoric ideal but a set of everyday practices that require intentionality, sacrifice, and creativity. It is taking seriously the life and teachings of Jesus and living them out in the complex and often conflicted realities of our world. This is discipleship.

Because we are committed to the holistic formation of peacemakers who will wage peace for the long haul, we want to identify three obstacles to contending in the realities of everyday life.

Commitment to convenience. There is nothing convenient about peacemaking. It is not fun nor easy, and it rarely fits into our hectic lives. There was nothing convenient about walking with our neighbor Lola in the realities of everyday life, yet this relationship was our call, and inconvenience is the call of all peacemakers who choose to walk in the way of Jesus.

When we become slaves to convenience, we miss out on joining God in his best work. We would argue that the terms "convenience" and "inconvenience" don't exist in the peacemaker's vocabulary. Now, we aren't saying we have to chase after every injustice under the sun, but we are saying we have to keep our eyes, hearts, and actions open to the areas where God is calling us to contend within in our spheres of influence. We will discuss what margins and boundaries might look like as peacemakers in chapter eight.

Here are a few questions to consider:

- How often do you find yourself "inconvenienced" by the plight of others?
- On a scale of one to ten, with ten being "ultimate priority," where would you place your own convenience?
- How do you imagine this interrupts your ability to contend?

Being "polite." A common perception of peacemakers is that they are passive pushovers. We argue that peacemakers are called to be the exact opposite as they move toward the center of conflict armed with transforming initiatives that expose evil and reassign dignity. To do this means we can't let our politeness get in the way of standing in front of the bulldozers that flatten people.

We have found that the root of slavery to politeness is image management and the fear of tarnishing our sparking reputations. Because we don't want to offend or upset the status quo, we create internal excuses that get us off the hook of constructive engagement. Not only is this bad news for those being abused, it doesn't allow us to live into who we were created to be or to join God in his work of reconciliation.

A couple of questions:

- When was the last time you needed to contend but didn't because you were too polite?
- What issues are you are being called to contend within that you have been avoiding out of fear of lost reputation?

Independence and isolation. In a culture that celebrates independence and autonomy, it's easy to assume that our personal flourishing doesn't impact the flourishing of others, whether those on our street or elsewhere in the world. That simply isn't true. Everything we do ripples positively or negatively toward others. Whether it's how we vote on issues on our neighborhood council, the amount of products and food we consume, or the way we speak of those who are different from us, our actions directly affect those far beyond our immediate circles. We are linked to one another. An embodiment of this reality is the African concept of *ubuntu*, which literally translates, "I am because we are."

Recently an American anthropologist conducted a study of African culture. He gathered a group of children and asked them all to assemble on one side of a room. On the other side of the room he placed a basket of fresh fruit and then offered these instructions to the children: "As soon as I say 'go,' the first person to run across the room and arrive at the basket of fruit gets all the fruit to themselves." The anthropologist then stepped back and counted down to "go."

Rather than breaking into individual sprints across the room, the children grabbed hands and walked together, as one, to the fruit. The anthropologist, dumbfounded, asked, "Why did you do this?"

One of the kids answered, "How can one of us be happy if the rest of us are sad?"

A few questions:

- How might our contending for others be impacted if we saw our flourishing as directly connected to theirs?

- In what areas of your life do you live out this value?

- In what areas of your life and practice can you can begin to reorient around this value?

BECOMING EVERYDAY PEACEMAKERS
WHO CONTEND

In the end, this peacemaking practice of contending is helpful only if it is embodied. There are many beautiful and helpful theories and ideas around peacemaking, but they must inform the way we live, love, and lead within our local and global communities. Contending requires that we neither run from conflict nor enter into it violently, but that we move toward it transformatively. In the face of violence—whatever form that may take—we don't get even; we get creative in love.

We would encourage you to take some time to identify a few conflicts or areas of brokenness in your life and begin to consider what actions you will take to contend creatively and constructively.

In the same way that Jesus contended for our flourishing, to the point of death on a cross, may we live into our call as everyday peacemakers who don't get even but get creative in love. And in a society where broken systems are breaking people, may we be everyday peacemakers who stand together with others in front of every kind of bulldozer that flattens people.

REFLECT AND DISCUSS

1. What framework for engaging conflict have you inherited in your tradition (just war, pacifism, just peacemaking), and how has that informed your practice as a peacemaker?

2. What obstacle limits you from contending creatively in the conflicts in your life?

3. What are some tangible ways you can begin to contend with creative love in our conflicted world?

EIGHT

RESTORE

The city of Bethany was a place of restoration. Within its boundaries stood the family home of Mary, Martha, and Lazarus, close friends of Jesus. As is true for all of us, restoration occurs when we find ourselves at home with those we love. We become more fully alive as we let our hair down and eat, rest, and play with those who are most life-giving to us. When the Scriptures tell of the interactions between Jesus and these three siblings, we're left to imagine this level of restorative intimacy between them.

But restoration took on another form among these four as well. It had to. As John tells the story, Lazarus had become ill and so the sisters sent for Jesus.

> The sisters sent word to Jesus, "Lord, the one you love is sick."
> When he heard this, Jesus said, "This sickness will not end in death. No, it is for God's glory so that God's Son may be glorified through it." Now Jesus loved Martha and her sister and Lazarus. So when he heard that Lazarus was sick, he stayed where he was two more days. (John 11:3-6)

The illness ended up taking Lazarus's life, and while Jesus was not there, somehow he knew what had happened. In a conversation with his disciples about whether or not to go to Judea, a place dangerous for him and his followers, Jesus said:

> "Our friend Lazarus has fallen asleep; but I am going there to wake him up."
> His disciples replied, "Lord, if he sleeps, he will get better." Jesus had been speaking of his death, but his disciples thought he meant natural sleep.
> So then he told them plainly, "Lazarus is dead." (John 11:11-14)

While the disciples were terrified to make the journey, Jesus was confident that the restoration that was about to occur in Bethany would change the lives of many.

When Jesus finally arrived, he discovered that Lazarus had already been entombed for four days and that the mourning process was in full swing. John continues the story with Martha running to meet Jesus:

> "Lord," Martha said to Jesus, "if you had been here, my brother would not have died. But I know that even now God will give you whatever you ask."
> Jesus said to her, "Your brother will rise again." (John 11:21-23)

Understanding Jesus to be referring to the resurrection of the dead on the last day, she agreed with him. But Jesus was not referring to a one-day resurrection. He was referring to a today restoration. Jesus said to Martha:

> "I am the resurrection and the life. The one who believes in me will live, even though they die; and whoever lives by believing in me will never die. Do you believe this?"

"Yes, Lord," she replied, "I believe that you are the Messiah, the Son of God, who is to come into the world."

After she had said this, she went back and called her sister Mary aside. "The Teacher is here," she said, "and is asking for you." (John 11:25-28)

In the interaction between Mary and Jesus we discover a growing relational divide caused by Jesus' delay. John places Mary at the feet of Jesus with these words: "Lord, if you had been here, my brother would not have died" (John 11:32). So moved was Jesus by her pain that he asked to be led to the place where Lazarus's body lay. When they arrived, Jesus wept while doubt about his power began to circulate among the watching crowd. They wondered why the one who could heal sight couldn't have kept this sick man alive (John 11:35-37). While the crowds speculated, Jesus prepared for restoration.

"Take away the stone," he said.

"But, Lord," said Martha, the sister of the dead man, "by this time there is a bad odor, for he has been there four days."

Then Jesus said, "Did I not tell you that if you believe, you will see the glory of God?"

So they took away the stone. Then Jesus looked up and said, "Father, I thank you that you have heard me. I knew that you always hear me, but I said this for the benefit of the people standing here, that they may believe that you sent me."

When he had said this, Jesus called in a loud voice, "Lazarus, come out!" The dead man came out, his hands and feet wrapped with strips of linen, and a cloth around his face.

Jesus said to them, "Take off the grave clothes and let him go." (John 11:39-44)

The unthinkable had happened. Jesus spoke life into Lazarus. Just as Jesus had promised, restoration was a reality that day. A life was restored. Broken hearts were restored. The circle of friends was restored. Hope in Jesus as the Messiah was restored. Resurrection occurred in Bethany and it restored all that was broken.

RESTORATION IS STILL HAPPENING IN BETHANY

If you were to go to Bethany today, you could visit Lazarus's empty tomb and be awestruck by the resurrection that occurred two millennia ago. And then you could walk three blocks to the home of our friends Milad and Manar, two Christian Palestinian peacemakers, and learn from them how Bethany is still a place of restoration.

Previously, generations of struggle between Israelis and Palestinians had made life nearly intolerable for those in this once thriving city. Where the streets used to ring with the sounds of music and laughter, they were now mostly quiet, interrupted only by sounds of fighting. Where youth once had the freedom of play, the restrictions placed on them had calcified their imaginations. Homemade guns had replaced soccer balls and musical instruments as their preferred toys.

Milad and Manar listened long and saw the despair. As they immersed into the lives of their neighborhood kids, they discovered that funding for the arts, music, theater, and sports was nonexistent in the United Nations-run schools. There were no opportunities for the emerging generation to channel their frustration in constructive, creative ways. Further, they discovered that the void of art and sports was enhancing the young people's experience of individualism, power accumulation, and personal protection. They concluded that what they were hearing and observing on the streets of their neighborhood was the death of hope and the disintegration of their society.

At this point Milad and Manar were not professional human-itarians with a crazy dream for a restored city. They were people of faith who lived in a hurting city. They didn't consider them-selves everyday peacemakers or citywide influencers. They didn't have access to wealthy Westerners to fund projects, nor did they have a large platform on which to stand and tell the story of what they were seeing. What they had was a living room, a few musical instruments, and a soccer ball. They had the respect of their neighbors, the admiration of the neighborhood kids, and some training in sports and the arts. The tools of restoration were in their hands before they knew what was broken and far before a dream for a restored Bethany emerged.

These two courageous Jesus-followers began to put the tools in their hands to use. They contended for the neighborhood kids by launching an after-school program that taught music and soccer. The program began with a dozen kids and quickly increased to over a hundred. Before long, hundreds of Bethany's kids packed onto their property wanting to be near their heroes and to be trained in music, art, and sports.

Space, time, and finances quickly became an issue. With the rapid growth of their initiative, Milad's salary was no longer enough to support his family and their work. But rather than releasing their dream, Milad and Manar got creative. They se-cured a larger gathering space and were discovered and funded by the Japanese government. Soon thereafter, Milad quit his highly sought-after job in the Old City to wholeheartedly pursue the work that lay in front of them.

A vocation of restoration hijacked Milad and Manar's life. Music, theater, and sports became the means by which healing took place. Restoration sprang to life because they made a series of decisions to use what they had to join God in ushering in the new world he was making. While they still live in the shadow of the separation wall, over time the sounds in the streets have shifted from argument to music and the games have transitioned from war back to soccer. Just like before, God's work of restoration is taking place in Bethany, and Milad and Manar are a part of it.

RESTORATION AS A PRACTICE?

While we identify restoration as the fourth practice of everyday peacemaking, we want to point out that it's less something we do and more something we get to be a part of. Remember, ours is the God whose mission is peacemaking (2 Corinthians 5:18-20). God has taken the initiative to restore the severed relationships among us. God bled so that that we could be whole, alive, and reconciled again (Colossians 1:19-20). God is actively making all things new, stronger, and more beautiful than before shalom was shattered (Revelation 21:5). God made peace possible and now invites us to join him in making it real (John 20:19-23). Simply put, restoration is what God gave his life for, and he invites us to spend our lives joining him in it.

As we see, immerse, and contend, we are actively joining God in bringing restoration to life in our interpersonal relationships, issues of local injustice, and international conflicts. But how do we do it and, when restoration springs to life, what does it look like?

JONO AND LAUREN'S STORY

Passion, resolve, and hospitality are the words I (Jer) would use to describe my friends Jono and Lauren. Their relationship reflects the beauty and strength of Kintsugi pottery because of their intentional commitment to pursue restoration.

As newlyweds, Jono and Lauren were given a down payment on their Bay Area home as a gift from a family member. They entered into a less-than-ideal home loan, but they weren't concerned as the economy was good and Jono was a well-compensated, award-winning video editor for a successful media organization.

The initial cracks in their relationship emerged when the economy crashed and took the housing market with it. Jono watched his company struggle as business dried up and his team diminished in size. At the same time, their unstable home loan shifted, more than doubling their monthly payment. Adding to the strain, Lauren had just downsized her workload as they welcomed their first child into the world.

The outlook was dire, money was drying up quickly, they could no longer afford their mortgage, and, with a newborn, sleep wasn't an option. Trust dissipated and blame increased between them. Civility was often absent, and simple conversations became emotionally painful arguments.

Blow by blow the cracks in this young marriage quickly widened into vast divides.

The good news is that God inhabits the dark places and the divides. His restorative wingspan reaches to the depths of our pain, conflict, and isolation. Jono and Lauren heard God's subtle voice from the depths compelling them to ask for help.

I was surprised yet inspired when they called me with a unique invitation. "We're going to have a fight," they said. "And we need you here."

They had realized they needed a guide to help them navigate the tricky waters of conflict. They recognized that they were using their tools to wound rather than heal. They needed help listening to and caring for one another through the pain for restoration to spring to life in their relationship.

In their request for guidance, Jono and Lauren exemplify an important peacemaking principle: rather than stumbling into restoration, we must take the initiative to create space for God, the great Kintsugi artist, to bring about restoration. This young couple did this first by forging trusting relationships before the divides widened. Both Jono and Lauren trusted me to be a champion for their relationship rather than a biased teammate with a preference for one over the other. Second, despite the pain, they recognized that the tools they had were limited and their attempts at restoration were falling short. They knew they needed help and, instead of hiding behind trees and fig leaves, they brought their pain into the light. Third, and most importantly, with all their attempts at restoration failing, Jono and Lauren were deeply convicted that God, whose name is shalom, was the only one who could mend the divides in their relationship with solid gold.

So I joined them at their dinner table on a beautiful midweek afternoon and we prayed together. We prayed for a long time before they invited me into their beautiful mess. It was saturated with misunderstanding, best intentions, unspoken expectations, disappointments, intentionally and inadvertently inflicted pain, and lots and lots of words.

Our conversation that day was a catalyst for forgiveness that eventually led to interpersonal restoration between Jono and Lauren. Today, golden scars remind them of God's restoration. Their relationship is stronger and more beautiful than before the break. And as one they are tangibly impacting their kids, their neighborhood, their city, and the thousands of people every year who step foot into the conference center they direct.

FORGIVENESS: NOT RESTORATION, BUT A GOOD START

We often mistakenly believe that restoration is forgiveness. From our earliest childhood memories we recall being coerced into saying, "I'm sorry!" for the slightest infraction. "I forgive you!" was the learned response, after which we were taught to get on with building our Lego towers. The assumption was that this exchange, if repeated consistently, would lead us to acknowledge our complicity in others' pain, immediately seek forgiveness, and, when the tables were turned, offer forgiveness without a second thought.

Very infrequently was there training on how to deal with the residual pain and lingering distrust caused by the conflict. So instead of developing into men and women who can walk a pathway all the way to restoration, we've become efficient at ignoring, dismissing, or "forgetting about" the pain. We in turn teach people to move around conflict rather than through it to restoration.

In Jono and Lauren's story, forgiveness did not immediately result in restoration. It was the catalyst that initiated healing and ushered in transformation. Forgiveness was the humble, courageous act that allowed God to begin joining the broken pieces together again. Forgiveness rebuilt trust such that the Spirit could begin mending the divides in gold.

Forgiveness is the gateway to reconciliation. As we see, immerse, and contend on the far side of forgiveness, we join God in his work of restoration.

EVIDENCE OF RESTORATION

But how do we know when an interpersonal relationship has been restored? What's the evidence that proves that the friendship is stronger and more beautiful than before it was broken? We've found that there are two constant and critical realities that help us recognize interpersonal restoration: (1) deepened intimacy and (2) reintegration into a co-creating community.

Can you think of a time when you've navigated a significant interpersonal conflict successfully? It might have been with a sibling, a good friend, a neighbor, or a spouse. Do you remember the discomfort you felt in the midst of the divide and how you obsessed about what you'd like to say if only you had the courage? Do you remember how you got sick to your stomach if you thought there was a chance you'd bump into each other?

And then, do remember the conversation where you sorted it out, where the infractions were appropriately owned, and where forgiveness was granted? Do you remember the release and liberation of that moment? You were on your way back to where you were—or so you thought.

Then there was that next time you were together. Perhaps you felt uncertainty mixed with hope that the forgiveness had stuck. And within that dissonance you had to make a decision for the relationship. You probably recognized that things weren't yet where they had been before. But you had a hunch that if you kept moving forward, your relationship could journey beyond even that level to a deeper, more intimate space.

This is why we identify conflict as the most fertile laboratory for relationships to flourish. Relationships are certainly strengthened when we experience success, but when we move all the way through conflict together, the journey forges new levels of trust and intimacy. Making it through the good times forges wonderful memories, but navigating conflict well, even beyond the apology, grows our intimacy and confidence that we can handle anything together.

However, the experience of confident intimacy is not an end unto itself. Whether in marriage or friendship, the end of intimacy is the co-creation of something beautiful. We know we're experiencing true restoration when, on the other side of conflict, we can identify each other's best contribution and call on each other to bring everything we are and have to the table.

This is the second piece of evidence of a restored relationship and is what we experience with God. His work on the cross and through the empty tomb restored our severed relationships and reintegrated us into his family. As a result, newfound levels of intimacy are possible and we live in belovedness as God's sons and daughters. But an equal reality is that we've been reintegrated as co-contributors, co-creators, and collaborators toward a just, mutually beneficial, restored future that Jesus referred to as the kingdom of God. The evidence of God's restorative work is that he reintegrates former enemies into a co-creating family tasked with joining God in bringing restoration to life in our world.

RESTORATION IN THE GOOD SAMARITAN

Returning one final time to our parable, we discover restoration occurring among four groups of people. The first is the most obvious. A victim of a vicious crime was physically, emotionally, and mentally traumatized. He was in desperate need of medical attention and fully dependent on another person to make life-saving decisions on his behalf.

In the merciful action of the Good Samaritan, we see the beginnings of the victim's restoration to health. The Samaritan brought him to an inn. No doubt he had to explain what had occurred on the Jericho road and what he had been able to do with his limited resources. Then he involved the innkeeper in the man's healing and committed the finances required to see restoration all the way through.

If we were to imagine this story continuing beyond Jesus' conclusion, it would be safe to assume that restoration cost a lot of time and money and required the contribution of a community of unlikely people.

Next, we must remember that Jesus shared this parable in response to a real question from a real person. A specific kind of restoration was needed in the life of the young lawyer, and Jesus' story likely hit its mark. It is here that we find the beginnings of a second restoration.

The questions the young lawyer asked uncover his longing for a pro-Jewish, anti-"other" God. They expose his preference for a conveniently homogenous existence that would extend throughout eternity. Jesus' story confronted these biases and assumptions. It tilled the soil of the young man's soul to the point where he had to admit that the "other" was his true neighbor. While he couldn't bring himself to name the Samaritan, he recognized that the one he had deemed furthest from God was, in fact, the one most like God. The mustard seeds of restoration had been planted and would take root only as the young man put into practice what he had learned from Jesus.

A third restoration that we can imagine is that which occurred among those who listened to the story. Perhaps sprinkled throughout the crowd were a handful of impoverished Jericho-road perpetrators, desperate men and women who survived by viewing pilgrims as objects to exploit. There were also likely several religious leaders within earshot of Jesus' story that day. These were men who lived in the disintegration of belief and practice and who misunderstood faithfulness as following rules that kept them at a safe distance from the world's pain.

There's a chance that former Jericho road victims stood listening to Jesus' story, reliving some of the most traumatic moments of their lives. These men and women may have carried physical and emotional scars and lived self-induced sentences of unforgiveness. It's also likely that a civic leader or two heard Jesus' story that day and looked down in shame at the mention of the violence. They were men who had known for years that economic disparity had contributed to the broken road in their community, yet they hadn't done anything about it.

As the story unfolded, perhaps the sight of the violent perpetrators who listened in was restored and they began to recognize the humanity, dignity, and image of God in themselves and those they had victimized. Perhaps restoration began for the faith leaders as the actions of the despised Samaritan were revealed as the most godly display of faithfulness. It's possible that the scars of former Jericho road victims began to turn "gold" as the story initiated them onto a journey of forgiveness. It's even possible that the seeds of restoration began to occur within the civic leaders that resulted in a resolve to address economic disparity and fix broken roads.

Finally, we get to the fourth focus of Jesus' restoration. This one is very personal. It's personal because his focus is on us. Like many who listened to this story two thousand years ago, we find ourselves undone by the exploitation of the perpetrators, the apathy of the religious, and the courageous compassion of the Samaritan. Rather than identifying with one of the people groups, we find ourselves at times mirroring all three of them. Jesus told stories like these to till up the parts of us that don't yet look and sound like him and to restore us to the best possible versions of ourselves.

What has the telling of parable of the Good Samaritan throughout this book begun to restore in you? Is the restoration occurring in you connected to your understanding of faithfulness? Are you beginning to see those you have categorized as existing beyond the redemptive reach of God? Perhaps your identity is being restored as God's beloved—maybe even your vocation as beloved reconcilers?

When we're listening well to the words of Jesus, restoration inevitably springs to life.

LOCAL RESTORATION: THE AIDS GROVE STORY

December 1, 2008, was a cold, rainy Monday. My (Jer's) daughter was a few days from turning one, and I had the day off to spend with her. My church had been involved in forging a relationship with a Ugandan organization that worked with AIDS orphans, so I knew that December 1 was World AIDS Day. I felt compelled to commemorate the day by standing in solidarity with those in our world who have been impacted by HIV/AIDS, so I opened the paper to see if there was a ceremony the two of us could attend.

I learned of a place in San Francisco's Golden Gate Park called the National AIDS Memorial Grove. A ceremony was to begin within the hour so I packed up my little girl and together we headed into the city. I did not expect that this chance encounter would begin the process of restoration between the local HIV/AIDS community and the local faith community.

When we arrived at the park, we discovered the hidden jewel that is the Grove. With our rain gear on and with my daughter packed on my back, we immersed into what felt like a sacred space. Embedded within the Grove was a white tent, and as we entered we felt as though we'd just stumbled into a family reunion, complete with the smells of warm food and the affection of people who loved one another. Rather than the HIV/AIDS community resembling the widows and orphans of Uganda, the demographic was largely white gay men. The stigmas and stereotypes that had been embedded in me throughout my Midwestern evangelical Christian upbringing immediately surfaced. No sooner had we entered the tent than I was looking for the exit.

We couldn't leave, though. We had been shown to a seat and the man behind the microphone was sharing the story of when AIDS ravaged San Francisco. He told stories of pain, resilience, rejection, and hope. My head jerked up when he commented on the local Christian church. To my dismay, rather than telling stories of unprecedented hospitality and extravagant love, he lamented how many church doors had remained closed and locked to their cries for help, even as his friends were dying on their doorsteps.

The commemoration concluded at the Circle of Friends. Similar to the Vietnam Wall, the circle enshrines the names of those lost to AIDS on a limestone floor. As I held the hands of the people on either side of me, I listened as they spoke the names of their beloved friends who had died of AIDS. I listened because I was curious, but also because I knew no one who had died of AIDS. I had no name—no life—to mourn. I had not been close enough to this group of people to be personally impacted by their pain.

I realized in that moment that I had spent my leadership trying to connect my people to the plight of the HIV-impacted community on the other side of the world to the exclusion of the impacted community in my local context. So focused were we on the international pandemic that we had failed to see that our own location was ground zero for HIV/AIDS in North America. Further, because our local HIV/AIDS-impacted community was also the LGBTQ community, I had to deal with the painful realization that I had been trained to not see them. Because I didn't see them, I was unaware of the severed divide between the local church and the LGBTQ community.

As I shared these thoughts with my leadership team later that week, we all felt the stuff of conviction. We sensed that Jesus was talking to us about our blindness. We needed our sight and our hearts healed and we figured that Jesus would use those I had met in the Grove as a part of our restoration. We began by immersing into their sacred space, the Grove, as participants in a monthly workday. The work was landscaping, but the real project was relationship building. Relationship was where our own restoration and that of those marginalized by us could occur.

For years we kept showing up—not as heroes, but as learners and friend makers. Our participation in workdays turned into dynamic friendships and, ultimately, into unique collaborations that successfully expanded the HIV/AIDS conversation beyond the LGBTQ community to embrace and support other vulnerable people groups who were suffering because of the disease. Our advocacy resulted in impoverished inner city women getting the attention, care, and support they desperately needed.

Six years later, on the eve of World AIDS Day, I had invited my friend and executive director of the AIDS Grove, John Cunningham, to speak at my church. I invited him to share the story of AIDS as it had ravaged San Francisco. I also asked him to share his own story as a gay HIV-positive man and to encourage and challenge the people of my church to keep joining God in the work of restoration. Before he arrived, he disclosed that he had been invited to speak in front of Congress and even at the White House, but he had never once been invited to speak in a church. He was as nervous as I had been when I entered the white tent six years earlier.

When he arrived that evening, he saw more than fifty people he already knew. This community had shown up early to welcome him because they wanted the first fifty faces John saw to be those of friends. He was immediately at home with us. He opened his remarks that night by saying this: "You have faithfully joined me in my sanctuary for the past six years. It is overdue for me to join you in yours."

One year later John invited me to speak and pray at the World AIDS Day commemoration. In his introduction, he commented on how his perspective of God, Jesus, pastors, and Christians had been restored because of our relationship. Before I took the stage, John asked this question in front of the five hundred who gathered: "Jer, when did *you and I* become *us*?" After seven years, the pronouns were shifting. Restoration was happening for all of us.

Today, dozens of Bay Area churches are connected to the AIDS Grove community. As a result, the divide between the church and the LGBTQ community in San Francisco is beginning to be mended with gold.

SHIFTING THE FOCUS OF RESTORATION

A similar pronoun divide is apparent in John 8. In the story, an adulterous woman was thrown down at the feet of Jesus by a group of religious men. The line between "us" and "them" was clearly defined. She had been ostracized from the community while being quietly exploited by the wealthy and powerful for sex. With each violation of her body, another piece of her soul was cracked. By the time she lay in front of Jesus, she was but a handful of broken pieces. Perhaps she considered herself beyond restoration and was ready to meet a gruesome end so that the pain would stop.

While the eyes of the mob scanned back and forth between the woman and the rocks in their hands, Jesus wrote in the dirt. The religious leaders were outraged by what seemed to be his indifference to the woman's sin and their violent faithfulness. Their bloodlust was justified in their Scriptures: this adulterous woman was a cause of faithlessness within the family and deserved death (Deuteronomy 22:22; Leviticus 20:10). They were so outraged by her sin that not only did they disregard her humanity and dignity, they also failed to seize her male companion who, according to the same Scriptures, deserved death by stoning as well.

In their damaged sight, she was beyond restoration. Her death sentence was justified by Scripture and it was about to be enacted by them, the faithful few.

As the group worked to decipher Jesus' penmanship on the canvas of dirt, Jesus invited the sinless among them to throw the first stone (John 8:7). And so the seeds of restoration were planted within the potential stone throwers—they knew that their sin meant they deserved a similar fate. If the soil of their souls was fertile, then over time their understanding of God, self, enemy love, and grace would be restored. Accompanying that restoration would be the renovation of their lives' practices.

The stones dropped and the accusers walked away. It was then that the focus of God's restorative work shifted to the broken beloved in front of him. He sat with her in her shame, fear, and confusion. He spoke to her as an equal as he picked up and gently held the pieces of her life. As he did, God began to restore her into the best possible version of herself.

Jesus took the religious mob's passion for faithfulness and shifted it toward their own needed restoration. Then he focused on the restoration necessary in the life of the woman who sat before him.

Here lies an essential peacemaking principle: rather than focusing on the restoration we want to see in others, we must demand our own ongoing restoration. Everyday peacemakers are men and women who commit to ongoing theological renovation and the pursuit of uncommon friendships that shatter the ceiling of our theology, break the shackles of our gospel, and liberate us into cross-shaped, restorative practice. We will engage locally in the work of peacemaking. Then, alongside the marginalized, we will begin to wonder when "they" became "us." As we participate together with God in the restoration of local issues of injustice, pronouns will shift and we'll celebrate where and how the Spirit is continuing to restore all of us.

OPENING OUR DOORS TO THE WORLD

Whenever we begin a conversation about restoration at an international level, we're met with pessimism. Questions surface like, "How does someone like me living in Des Moines, Iowa, join God in the work of international peacemaking?" In questions like these we discover just how disconnected many of us are from how globalization, international conflict, and the immigration phenomenon have brought global communities into our own neighborhoods.

While it's likely that most of us will never find ourselves in international peace negotiations, almost all of us are relationally connected to the divides in our world through our neighbors, our businesses, our churches, and even our social media channels. But how do we leverage those relationships? And in so doing, how do we join in God's work of restoration on a global scale?

Andy, Jamie, and their kids are your typical white evangelical family. They're natives of Seattle, Washington, and local practitioners of international peacemaking. Refugees from Iraq and Syria inhabit their neighborhood, creating an opportunity for their family to become an instrument of peace in our war-torn world.

The reality of ISIS paired with the chaos of the Syrian conflict has created a refugee crisis the likes of which hasn't been experienced since World War II. At the time we are writing this, 4.6 million Iraqis have been displaced due to ISIS campaigns. According to the Internal Displacement Monitoring Centre, 6.1 million Syrians have been internally displaced while an additional 4.8 million Syrians are on a perilous refugee journey toward safety.

The state of Washington is considered one of the top ten most receptive states to refugees in the country with the Seattle area leading the way. To date, more than fifteen thousand Iraqi refugees have been resettled in the greater Seattle area and between thirty and fifty thousand Syrians. Andy, Jamie, and their kids are at the center of an international peacemaking effort in their own neighborhood.

As it always does, it began with healed sight. Neither Andy nor Jamie had been to Iraq or Syria nor had they spent much time with Muslims. They simply saw in the local newspapers that a group of Middle Eastern refugees were moving to town and were in desperate need of support and accompaniment. Reality hit Andy and Jamie. Their new international neighbors needed help adjusting to life in a new country after unthinkable trauma in their own.

Their immersion began with a cultural competency training offered by a local refugee resettlement organization. Within days, an Iraqi family was living with them in their small apartment. Hospitality was the tool of their contending. While Andy and Jamie didn't have much, they did have a spare bedroom, some extra folding chairs, and the resources to ensure that their dinner table had enough food for everyone. They also had a network of friends and family that pitched in additional resources to ensure that all who called their humble apartment "home" had what they needed.

Andy and Jamie worked hard to help their new roommates get acquainted with an American kitchen, local grocery stores, the school system, and public transportation. English lessons were organic as, around the shared table, they worked with their foreign friends to establish a baseline understanding of English. Over time, a trusting relationship developed that created the space for healing to occur for the Iraqi family. But theirs wasn't the only restoration that occurred.

We have reflected with Andy on the experience of welcoming refugees, and he's been quick to declare that the restoration that's occurring is his own. His understanding of who God is and who God is for is expanding. He's been forced to acknowledge how he's allowed his upbringing, theological development, and media influences to blind him from people who are not like him. As their home has become a place of immersion, he's learned how God inhabits the spaces Andy formerly protected and how God brings about holistic restoration when we release our grip on "our" resources. He and his family are working hard to confront their constructions of "enemy" and are finding that as they practice creative love, God is restoring them, those they host, and those who are on the journey with them.

Since hosting that original family, Andy and his family have hosted eight additional Iraqi and Syrian families in their home. We have shared their story with faith, civic, and political leaders throughout the country as an example of how to engage in international peacemaking with our refugee neighbors. Andy, Jamie, and their kids are joining in God's work of international restoration from their living room and dinner table and, as a result, others are learning to do the same.

RESTORATION TAKES MYRIAD FORMS

As we learn to see, immerse, and contend, we actively join God in bringing restoration to life in our interpersonal relationships, issues of local injustice, and international conflicts. Often, the restoration that springs to life in us and those around us surprises us. Restoration realized takes shape in hundreds of different ways.

It looks like our friends Ben (Israeli Jew) and Moira (Palestinian Muslim), who were formerly enemy neighbors but who now co-create a mutually beneficial future by teaching all of the children of their divided land to choose love over fear. It looks like our Palestinian-Israeli friend Jamal, who offers vocational training, counseling, and rehabilitation support for the recently incarcerated in his city. It looks like our friend Teresa who, through San Francisco's Old Skool Café, reintegrates formerly incarcerated kids and at-risk youth into society as creative, entrepreneurial contributors. It looks like our Mexican friend Samuel who created a simple set of raised garden beds called Bordo Farms to remind deported men of their dignity and value and create jobs as they find their way. Restoration looks like our friend

Gilberto, who serves thousands of migrants and deportees in Tijuana through counseling, career coaching, networking, job searches, and room and board, giving those on the move the toeholds they need to pursue a flourishing future.

Restoration looks like what is happening at the National AIDS Memorial Grove as the gay community and the faith community—unlikely friends—walk toward one another in love and join God in each other's healing. It looks like men and women walking the kill zone of East Oakland on Friday nights with our friend Ben to decrease gun-related violence through peaceful, relational presence.

Restoration looks like our friend Michelle, who is accompanying her friend all the way through her dangerous addiction to freedom. Restoration is what happened as Jono and Lauren walked all the way through past hurt such that the divides in their relationship were mended with pure gold.

Restoration looks like Connor, the fatherless kid in my neighborhood, flourishing in school, growing in confidence, learning to throw and catch a baseball, and embracing his belovedness by me and, ultimately, by God. It looks like a derelict side yard turned into a neighborhood garden oasis where Gail could co-create beautiful things and find belonging again.

The restored world that God is making—that we get to join him in ushering in—looks like a world where brothers no longer kill their brothers and where women and children are no longer exploited for the pleasure of men. This restored world is one in which no human beings are owned by other, more powerful human beings.

The restored world God is making is one in which senseless gun violence no longer produces dead kids in our streets and where immigrants and refugees no longer hide in fear in the shadows of overcrowded apartments. It's a world where human

beings are no longer trapped in cages, where addiction no longer
has power, and where hunger and thirst no longer plague humanity. It's a world where children are no longer trapped in
systems without families.

Restoration happens when capitalism no longer trumps compassion, where consumption no longer trumps generosity, and
where my flourishing no longer trumps yours. It happens when
you and I assume the posture of the cross in myriad ways for the
benefit of others. Restoration springs to life when we leverage
and lay down our power and privilege so that others flourish.

This restored world that we speak of is made possible because
of the death and resurrection of Jesus. It's the new world that
God is making, and everyday peacemakers get to be a part of
bringing it about.

REFLECT AND DISCUSS

1. Sometimes restoration looks like a return to the way things
   were, and sometimes something brand new emerges. What
   are some stories of restoration that have unfolded in your
   interpersonal relationships and local contexts?

2. What kinds of international restoration have you had the
   privilege of being part of?

3. What have you done to tell, retell, and celebrate these stories
   of restoration as signposts of God's kingdom come?

4. What might restoration look like in the conflicts you are currently navigating in your everyday places?

NINE

TIME TO BEGIN

Remember that porch in the Rocky Mountains where our adventure began? Our mentor was convinced that once our vision for peace and peacemaking was grounded in Jesus, our embodiment of that vision would change the world.

That moment catalyzed a years-long journey that has taken us not only through the Scriptures but also around the world, through interpersonal, local, and global conflicts, and into uncommon friendships. As we've journeyed, a definition for peace has surfaced, as has a set of peacemaking practices.

Throughout it all we've had reason to laugh harder and cry more deeply. We've bled, sweated, lamented, and celebrated more than ever before. There have been times throughout the years when our attempts at peacemaking have failed miserably—moments when years of work toward restoration have crumbled because we or someone else chose, once again, to reach for the fruit of power rather than the hand of another. But there have also been moments of unthinkable joy as we've found ourselves participating with God and others in mending ragged divides with pure gold. An everyday peacemaking movement is springing to life and, as our mentor speculated, it's changing the world.

This, friends, is the adventure we've all been invited into. While we live on this side of shalom's restoration, there's still work to be done. Jesus himself had some everyday peacemaking to tend to in the wake of resurrection. Let's consider one final moment, this time in the life of the resurrected Jesus, where he pursued the holistic repair of a severed relationship.

At the end of John's Gospel (John 21) we find Peter, who had denied Jesus, dwelling in deepest despair. Just a few days had passed since Jesus had washed his feet and assigned extraordinary meaning to the bread and wine. It was around that Passover table that Jesus revealed that Peter would be the one to refute the reality of their friendship (John 13:18-30).

Just a few hours after dinner, still reeling from the shock of that revelation, Peter had drawn his sword in armed defense of Jesus. He was so committed to his rabbi that he swung his weapon at the head of the man arresting his leader. He intended to kill to prove his allegiance. Luckily, fear and rage altered his aim and the sword took an ear rather than a life (John 18:10). True to form, Jesus picked up the man's ear and put it back in place (Luke 22:51). It was just one more life-altering restoration before the ultimate restoration would occur.

When they arrested Jesus, Peter hid like a coward. Commitment to self-preservation and safety indeed trumped his allegiance to Jesus. A mix of curiosity and courage had brought Peter back into proximity with Jesus that night, but the questions of a young girl caused his courage to fail not once (John 18:15-18) but three times (John 18:25-27). His repeated betrayal severed the relationship.

After resurrection, Jesus encountered Peter and the others in a locked room. He was alive! It was an impossible and troubling and wonderful reality. Decisive peace had been waged, but it didn't seem like the peace was real between Peter and Jesus. On the other side of the resurrection, their relationship was still severed. Peter knew it and so did Jesus.

John placed Peter back in his own fishing boat a few days after that upper room encounter (John 21:1-19). It was a scene reminiscent of the moment when their relationship began (Luke 5:1-11). Just as had happened then, Jesus showed up on the beach and told the master fisherman how to fish. In that familiar moment Peter recognized the presence of Jesus, so he jumped out of the boat and swam to the scarred feet of his rabbi.

Despite the broken relationship, Jesus saw Peter. He saw Peter's pain and shame. As had always been the case, what Jesus saw stopped him dead in his tracks and became the most important thing in the world to him. Compassion fueled a familiar merciful action: Jesus set another table (John 21:12-14). Over breakfast he immersed deeper into Peter's insecurity. As he broke the bread and shared the cup, Jesus reminded Peter of the extent to which he had contented for Peter's restoration. With bread in scarred hand, Jesus extended forgiveness and the restoration between them began. That restoration would continue as Peter spent the rest of his life waging peace.

Friends, God's restoration continues to be realized in our world today as we embrace our vocation as everyday peacemakers. As we see, immerse, and contend, we are restored . . . others are restored . . . broken systems are transformed . . . and God's peace becomes real in our world.

YOUR TURN

Chances are good that we all will find ourselves in conflict with others, embedded within locations where all is not as it should be, and compelled toward international brokenness. As our journey nears its end, it's time for us to get very practical. Let's begin by becoming students of the conflicts we find ourselves within. Identifying these conflicts will help us more effectively listen to what the Spirit is saying about the peacemaking steps we can take to mend the divides with gold.

Identifying your interpersonal conflict. The rubber meets the road for everyday peacemakers in our relationships with those closest to us. For some, identifying that conflict is easy because strife with a family member, neighbor, or colleague is top of mind. For others, years of suppressing the conflict have caused the details to grow foggy. Whether simple or challenging, it's always a gut-wrenching process to identify the conflict and then recognize that each of us is, to one degree or another, both a victim and a perpetrator of the pain.

During one of our most recent Israeli-Palestinian Conflict Immersion Trips, one of our participants allowed herself to move through just such a process for the sake of a much-needed restoration. Marta was a seasoned follower of Jesus, a mother, a wife, and a spiritual director. Her presence within that particular Immersion Trip brought a calming stability that was evidence of a deep faith forged through pain, experience, and celebration.

As we journeyed together, she was undone by the complexity of the conflict in the Middle East while also inspired by the everyday peacemakers on the front lines. Unbeknownst to the rest of us, she was also being undone by the complexity of her own years-old conflict with a family member. The Spirit used the living parable of conflict at an international scale to reveal to her a severed interpersonal relationship that required her attention.

Ten days after our time together in Israel-Palestine, we hosted a coaching call where we asked each participant to identify one step, big or small, that they had taken toward healing a broken relationship. True to form throughout the Immersion Trip, Marta waited until the end to share her own story. It was simple but profound. She spoke of how the Spirit had used the immersion experience to reveal her role in the severed relationship and to invite her to see, immerse, and contend such that the broken relationship could one day be fully restored. For the first time in years, she took the initiative and opened a channel of communication. Marta is becoming an instrument of peace within her family.

What is your interpersonal conflict? Perhaps it's freshly severed and easy to identify. Or maybe its decades old and the severity of the pain has subsided, making it more difficult to identify. When you're honest with yourself, though, the ache of that conflict remains, along with disappointment that the relationship has never fully recovered.

Is your conflict with an immediate family member, a former friend, a neighbor, a boss, a colleague? What happened and how did it change your perspective of the other person? Of yourself? Of God? Is your sight in need of healing? What step is the Spirit inviting you to take that will bring your closer to the conflict? How is the Spirit inviting you to contend for restoration?

Identifying a local injustice. The San Francisco Bay Area is an international hub of innovation. It is a fusion of breathtaking beauty, exceeding wealth, surging multiculturalism, and debilitating poverty. Undergirding the Bay Area lifestyle is a burgeoning population of documented and undocumented migrants. They live in the shadows in overcrowded apartments in impoverished neighborhoods and work long hours as landscapers, housecleaners, and dishwashers.

Becca was a social worker among the migrant community in her first job out of college and therefore was in touch with the painful realities of this hidden community. A member of a local church, Becca knew that faithfulness for her congregation required that they "show up" among their local migrant community.

But they didn't exactly know what "show up" meant, so Becca entered our Immigrants' Journey Immersion Trip.

In the initial phase of the lab, Becca began learning about immigration in her neighborhood. She read books and articles, participated in online interviews with national experts, heard from local practitioners, and viewed documentaries. She searched the Scriptures and began to develop a theology of an immigrant God who identifies hospitality toward foreigners as the defining mark of the family of God.

All of this learning reawakened in Becca her passion for the migrant community. Simultaneously she discovered just how vulnerable the migrants around her were, how insurmountable the resource gaps were becoming, and how painfully national immigration policy and enforcement were tearing families apart.

The watershed moment for Becca occurred when we found ourselves in the apartment of a migrant family. She was inspired by their resilience, creativity, and hospitality yet disoriented by the challenges and lack of resources making their life so difficult. As the Hispanic father shared his story of their migration and of making a home in the Bay Area, his faith affected Becca deeply. As she listened she learned about a God who would cross any border to find her and that faithfulness would require her to do the same on behalf of others. In one immersive encounter, a young migrant dad accompanied Becca into profound transformation and helped her understand what it meant to "show up."

Instead of swooping in like heroes from the young, wealthy, white church of the suburbs, Becca and her husband immersed themselves into authentic friendships with their migrant neighbors. The deeper they immersed, the more clearly they saw God, themselves, their friends, and the plight of the countless men, women, and children on the move in our world today. In the context of these new friendships, which included countless shared tables and long conversations, they discovered their own complicity and just how much their complacency impacted the local migrant community. As trust built, assumptions and premature conclusions held by both parties were confronted and reordered. Becca, along with her husband and her church, are becoming instruments of peace in the Bay Area as they contend with and for the flourishing of their migrant friends.

Who are the marginalized in your neighborhood? Is there a local injustice that keeps you up at night? Is there a surplus of kids trapped in a foster system without hope of a stable, loving family? Is there educational disparity based on income levels and ethnicity that channels resources toward select high-performing schools while others suffer? Is your neighborhood being gentrified by upwardly mobile, well-educated professionals? Are the minorities near you being displaced to the fringes by skyrocketing rents? Are people of color in your city being mistreated, exploited, even killed because of unjust policies and racial profiling? Are women in your area afforded the same vocational opportunities and salaries as their male colleagues?

What about the poor and the homeless? While they may be fed and clothed, who is accompanying them out of unhealthy habits and cycles of pain into a more hopeful future? What about the young women and children who are sexually exploited night after night? Who sees them, immerses into their pain, and contends for their freedom?

How have you been blinded to the plight of those who suffer in your local context? What next step is the Spirit inviting you to take to draw near the marginalized, misunderstood, and vulnerable? Are there champions already contending on the front lines of the pain and can you take a learning posture alongside them? How is God inviting you to begin the process of restoration in your neighborhood or city?

Identifying an international conflict. For more than a year
Jamie worked for an organization called Questscope in Jordan
that is committed to putting the last first. While she had
always been intrigued by the Middle East, her plan for her life
didn't necessarily include an extended living arrangement in
the Jordanian desert. She was a nurse with a tender heart and
a compassion that mobilized her toward people in pain.

The timing of her work in Jordan coincided with a surge of
violence in Syria that displaced millions. The population of the
Za'atari refugee camp was already oversaturated when Jamie first
accompanied her Jordanian colleagues among the rows of hap-
hazard homes. What she saw in the streets of Za'atari stopped
her dead in her tracks and become the most important thing in
the world to her.

Her mission was twofold: to capture the refugees' stories and
to find ways to communicate a message of hope and resilience in
the midst of extreme tragedy to a world that desperately needed
to hear it. The refugees were willing to reexperience unthinkable
trauma to share their stories, but Jamie wondered if the world
would be willing to listen. And if it did, what would hearing these
stories accomplish?

Just when her Jordanian colleagues had turned into confidants
and refugees had become dear friends, Jamie's role concluded and
she returned to a nursing career in Chicago. It was about that
time that Syrian refugees began pouring into Turkey, where they
boarded unstable boats for the perilous journey to Greece. While
Jamie, and many like her, had been trying to get the plight of the
Syrian refugees on the world's radar, it took one picture of an innocent little boy washed up on the shores of the Mediterranean
coast to accomplish it. The world woke up to the pain of the
people who Jamie loved.

Meanwhile, a world away from Za'atari, Jamie attended one of our workshops where the four practices of everyday peacemaking put language to the life she had been living in Jordan. She resolved in that workshop to continue a lifestyle of peacemaking in her own neighborhood: her first action step was to identify the local resettlement agencies that were working with Chicago-based Syrian refugees.

In no time Jamie was partnered as a mentor with a fourteen-year-old young Syrian woman who was struggling to find her way in the wake of trauma in the neighborhoods of Chicago. Jamie could resonate with the experience of displacement, and so these two women began to contend for one another. Just like in Jordan, the two women stumbled through the awkwardness of building a new friendship and over time built trust. That's when Jamie was granted access to the entire family and became one of them.

While some of us are compelled toward issues of local injustice, others of us have an international calling. In a globalized world, this yearning doesn't always require us to physically relocate.

Is there an international conflict that has captured your attention? Is it the plight of the millions of refugees who are being displaced because of war and psychological trauma? Is it the complexity of the Israeli-Palestinian conflict or the horror of the violence in the Congo? Are you broken by the use of rape as a tool of war or does your heart break for men, women, and children who are enslaved for the benefit of the powerful?

What about child soldiers? Have you seen the pictures and read the stories of communities trying to survive in the world's largest outdoor garbage dumps? Who sees the impoverished in Haiti or the civilians who are traumatized by ISIS? Who is immersed in their pain and is contending for their flourishing?

What do you need to read or watch so that you can see more clearly what's happening in our global village? Who can you

travel with in order to experience the beauty and the pain of a
new place and its people and learn from the embedded peacemaking practitioners? What next step is the Spirit inviting you
to take beyond financial investment that will continue God's
process of restoration in our world?

BUILDING A ROAD MAP

At the conclusion of every Global Immersion training initiative,
we invite our participants to carefully discern the practical steps
they must take. It's an essential process that synthesizes learning
into action and helps dreams become reality. This is the point
we've reached in this book. Up until this point we've played the
role of guides, but now the time has come for you to build your
road map for moving forward.

The most effective road maps we've seen created by everyday
peacemakers include three critical elements.

A desired destination. An effective road map first includes a
picture of restoration or progress toward restoration that in-
forms the steps to be taken. Whether interpersonal, local, or
international, what dream or picture has God given you for restoration? Write it down. And then, rather than assuming that
your picture of restoration is complete, get some input from the
person you're in conflict with (interpersonal), those who are
most negatively impacted by broken systems (local injustice), or
those who are suffering the consequences of conflict globally
(international conflict).

Clear timelines. A good road map also sets time-bound
goals for progress. We've found that intervals of ten days, ten
weeks, and ten months inspire both a sense of urgency and a
commitment to see the process through. While complete restoration may not be accomplished within ten days, ten weeks,
or ten months, this time frame helps create moments of

accountability, opportunities to assess and celebrate, and cal-endared moments in time where we can evaluate, reorient, and relaunch.

Realistic action items. Finally, the road map includes concrete steps to take within each time interval. We encourage you to get honest about the time it takes to pursue the holistic repair of severed relationships and broken systems. Choosing to be realistic in plotting out your map will keep you inspired to walk the road toward peace. We offer a guide for building your road map in the appendices as well as suggested practices to get you going.

As we develop our road maps, let's be careful not to disassociate the process from the guiding whisper of the Holy Spirit. Remember, no one is more committed to mending the divides than God. Therefore it's paramount that we listen for the Spirit's voice as we develop the map and then walk the road ahead. It's guaranteed that we will be surprised by the valleys, vistas, and detours the Spirit will guide us through. That's okay, for it is in the process of pursuing restoration that we find ourselves being restored. For more help to plan your route, turn to the resources in appendix A and let the road mapping begin.

COMMISSIONING

Two thousand years ago Jesus said, "Blessed are the peacemakers, for they will be called children of God" (Matthew 5:9).

Friends, blessed are you as you discover the humanity, dignity, and image of God in others.

Blessed are you as you learn to see the plight and pain of others as well as your own contribution to what is broken.

Blessed are you as you step off the road of comfort and immerse into the radical center of others' pain armed with compassion and curiosity.

Blessed are you as you spend your life getting creative in love.

As you live this way, you join an ancient community of everyday peacemakers who have participated with God in ushering in a restored world.

Toward that end we now go together.

ACKNOWLEDGMENTS

While there are far more people who have shaped us and this project than we can mention here, we want to acknowledge the sacred significance of our families, international peacemaking mentors, and Global Immersion teammates. More than fueling this project, each is fueling the movement of everyday peacemaking by living the content found on these pages. We are listening and committed to continue learning from and alongside each of you.

Appendix A

BUILDING A ROAD MAP:
TEN DAYS, TEN WEEKS, TEN MONTHS

Below are three sample road maps to give you some more ideas to plan your route. You'll note that our suggestions here lean toward the practices of seeing and immersing. Recognizing how to contend happens only after we've seen and immersed. Restoration is what happens as we see, immerse, and contend, so it's unrealistic to plot it out as ten-ten-ten practice. Instead we recommend that you begin the road mapping process by identifying the conflict you find yourself within or compelled by and asking these questions:

- What do I imagine full restoration looking like?

- What are the current issues of injustice or power abuse that will be no more?

- Who is currently indifferent, silent, silenced, sidelined, or working independently who will be collaborating on the front lines?

INTERPERSONAL RELATIONSHIPS

The rubber of everyday peacemaking meets the road in the context of interpersonal relationships. Use the framework below to establish a pathway toward interpersonal restoration.

Ten days. Identify the ways in which you have contributed to the relational divide or its widening. Open a channel of communication with that person through a handwritten letter that expresses your dissatisfaction with the relational distance and your desire to contribute to a restored relationship.

Ten weeks. Initiate an in-person conversation in which you learn about the other person's understanding of what happened. This should be a moment of deep curiosity where you ask probing questions and distance yourself from the need to be understood.

Ten months. Reestablish a rhythm of shared experiences (in person or online) where you have the time to navigate all the way through the conflict to a place of restoration.

LOCAL INJUSTICE

The social locations where we live, work, and play are wrought with unjust systems that benefit a few at a high cost to many others. The framework below will help you become a student of your place and guide you in peacemaking practices.

Ten days. Develop a reading and viewing list to actively learn about the injustice, whether it involves immigration, race relations, housing disparity, homelessness, human trafficking, or any number of issues resulting from broken local systems.

Ten weeks. Identify and establish a meeting with a local influencer who is immersed and contending for those most impacted by the issue of local injustice. Forge a friendship and begin the process of learning about the issue and the people involved from his or her perspective.

Ten months. Move from occasional volunteer to friend and from friend to ally of a person or family that has been maligned by the injustice. Seek to understand how you can accompany them and allow yourself to be accompanied by them.

INTERNATIONAL CONFLICT

You don't have to be a diplomat or professional humanitarian to engage in international peacemaking. The suggestions below will help you navigate a conflict from wherever you are on the globe.

Ten days. Discover and follow the embedded practitioners in that particular international conflict so you can learn from their perspective, read what they recommend, and develop a more robust understanding of the place, the people, and the conflict.

Ten weeks. Discover who in my local context is from that particular place or is connected to its violence. Set up a meeting to begin building a relationship where you can get more access to the conflict and the people being traumatized as a result.

Ten months. Identify an organization that will facilitate a trip to the region you've identified and that can grant access to seemingly inaccessible people and places within the international conflict.

NOW IT'S YOUR TURN

- The conflict I find myself in or that most compels me is . . .

- Full restoration would look like ...

- The current issues of injustice or power abuse that need to end are ...

- Some people who can collaborate on the front lines are ...

- In ten days I will ...

- In ten weeks I will ...

- In ten months I will ...

A PEACEMAKING LIBRARY

This is not a comprehensive list but a good place to start to learn more about everyday peacemaking.

Cleveland, Christena. *Disunity in Christ: Uncovering the Hidden Forces That Keep Us Apart*. Downers Grove, IL: InterVarsity Press, 2013.

Dear, John. *Thomas Merton, Peacemaker: Meditations on Merton, Peacemaking, and the Spiritual Life*. Maryknoll, NY: Orbis Books, 2015.

Henderson, Michael. *Forgiveness: Breaking the Chain of Hate*. Portland, OR: Arnica Publishing, 2003.

Katongole, Emmanuel. *Reconciling All Things: A Christian Vision for Justice, Peace, and Healing*. Downers Grove, IL: InterVarsity Press, 2008.

King, Martin Luther, Jr., *Strength to Love*. Minneapolis: Fortress, 2010.

Lederach, John Paul. *The Little Book of Conflict Transformation*. Intercourse, PA: Good Books, 2003.

———. *Moral Imagination: The Art and Soul of Building Peace*. New York: Oxford University Press, 2005.

Love, Rick. *Peace Catalysts: Resolving Conflict in Our Families, Organizations and Communities*. Downers Grove, IL: InterVarsity Press, 2014.

McNeil, Brenda Salter. *Roadmap to Reconciliation: Moving Communities into Unity, Wholeness and Justice.* Downers Grove, IL: InterVarsity Press, 2015.

Sider, Ron. *Nonviolent Action: What Christian Ethics Demands but Most Christians Have Never Really Tried.* Grand Rapids: Brazos Press, 2015.

Tutu, Desmund. *No Future Without Forgiveness.* New York: Image, 1999.

Volf, Miroslav. *Exclusion and Embrace: A Theological Exploration of Identity, Otherness, and Reconciliation.* Nashville: Abingdon Press, 1996.

Wink, Walter. *Jesus and Nonviolence: A Third Way.* Minneapolis: Augsburg Fortress, 2003.

Other authors worth exploring include

- Dorothy Day
- Adolfo Perez Esquivel
- Julian of Norwich
- Aung San Suu Kyi
- Albert Lithuli
- Riguberta Menchu
- Thomas Merton
- Parker Palmer
- Richard Rohr
- Oscar Romero
- Teresa of Ávila

NOTES

2 SPEAKING OF PEACE

21 *Rick Malouf is:* Conversation between Rick Malouf, Jon, and Jer at 4 Eagle Ranch in Vail, Colorado on September 17, 2013.

23 *shalom indicates wholeness:* Arthur A. Cohen and Paul Mendes-Flohr, *20th Century Jewish Religious Thought: Original Essays on Critical Concepts, Movements, and Beliefs* (Philadelphia: Jewish Publication Society, 2009), 701.

26 *That "something more":* John A. Powell and Stephen Menendian, "The Problem of Othering: Towards Inclusiveness and Belonging," Othering and Belonging, www.otheringandbelonging.org/the-problem -of-othering, accessed January 3, 2017.

29 *God would die:* Ray Vander Laan, "God With Us," That the World May Know, www.thattheworldmayknow.com/god-with-us-article, retrieved January 11, 2016. For more on ancient covenant making, see Sandra L. Richter, *The Epic of Eden: A Christian Entry into the Old Testament* (Downers Grove, IL: InterVarsity Press, 2008), 69-91.

3 THE DIVINE PATTERN

48 *Ninety percent of Americans:* Mark A. Schuster et al., "A National Survey of Stress Reactions After the September 11, 2001, Terrorist Attacks," *New England Journal of Medicine* 345 (2001): 1507-12.

4 EVERYDAY CONFLICT, EVERYDAY PEACEMAKING

53 *Spirituality is the process:* See Richard Rohr, *Breathing Under Water: Spirituality and the Twelve Steps* (Cincinnati: St. Anthony Messenger Press, 2011).

59 *conflict is the most dynamic laboratory:* John Paul Lederach, *The Little Book of Conflict Transformation* (Intercourse, PA: Good Books, 2003), 18.

64   *Lebanon, a nation of six million:* "Syria's Refugee Crisis in Numbers," Amnesty International, December 20, 2016, www.amnesty.org/en /latest/news/2016/02/syrias-refugee-crisis-in-numbers.

While we probably won't personally broker: International Rescue Committee (www.rescue.org) and World Relief (www.worldrelief.org) are great organizations to contact about supporting local refugees.

6 IMMERSE

91   *God would rather:* Stanley Hauerwas, seminary commencement address, Eastern Mennonite University, May 1, 2010, www.emu/now /podcast/tag/stanley-hauerwas.

100   *Brian McLaren argues:* Brian McLaren, *Why Did Jesus, Moses, the Buddha, and Muhammed Cross the Road?* (New York: Hachette Book Group, 2012).

7 CONTEND

110   *Without support, most deportees:* Alejandra Ortiz, in-person lecture, Tijuana, Mexico, 2014.

112   *Scholars argue:* "The Good Samaritan's Money," American Bible Society, bibleresources.americanbible.org/node/1489, accessed February 15, 2017.

115   *Never forget that justice:* Cornel West, "Cornel West Quotes," Goodreads, www.goodreads.com/author/quotes/6176.Cornel_West, accessed February 15, 2017.

If God commanded all people: Mae Cannon, *Social Justice Handbook* (Downers Grove, IL: InterVarsity Press, 2009), 32.

According to their study: Glen H. Stassen and David P. Gushee, *Kingdom Ethics: Following Jesus in Contemporary Context* (Downers Grove, IL: IVP Academic, 2003), 355.

116   *Peacemakers who see:* We appreciate the restorative justice framework offered by Howard Zehr in *Changing Lenses: Restorative Justice for Our Times* (Harrisonburg, VA: Herald Press, 2015).

118   *Just war theory became a framework:* Stassen and Gushee, *Kingdom Ethics*, 158.

119   *After an exhaustive study:* Ron Sider, *The Early Church on Killing: A Comprehensive Sourcebook on War, Abortion, and Capital Punishment* (Grand Rapids: Baker Academic, 2012).

122 *Biblical scholars have done extensive work:* See Richard B. Hays, *The Moral Vision of the New Testament: A Contemporary Introduction to New Testament Ethics* (New York: HarperOne, 1996), and Stassen and Gushee, *Kingdom Ethics.*

Jesus quickly reminds him: Stassen and Gushee, *Kingdom Ethics,* 156.

8 RESTORE

150 *4.6 million Iraqis:* Rick Gladstone, "1.2 Million Iraqis Could Be Uprooted in Mosul Battle, U.N. Says," *New York Times,* August 23, 2016, https://www.nytimes.com/2016/08/24/world/middleeast/isis-mosul-iraq.html.

According to the Internal Displacement Monitoring Centre: "Syria," Internal Displacement Monitoring Centre, www.internal-displacement.org/database/country/?iso3=SYR, accessed November 30, 2016.

an additional 4.8 million Syrians: "The Syrian Refugee Crisis and Its Repercussions for the EU," Syrian Refugees, European University Institute, September 2016, syrianrefugees.eu.

The state of Washington: Cambria Roth and Goorish Wibneh, "Washington Among Top 10 States for Refugees," Crosscut.com, April 22, 2016, crosscut.com/2016/04/refugees-united-nations-immigration-kelly-clements.

more than fifteen thousand Iraqi refugees: "Data on Immigrants and Refugees," Office of Immigrant and Refugee Affairs, Seattle.gov, www.seattle.gov/iandraffairs/data, accessed November 30, 2016.

between thirty and fifty thousand Syrians: Nina Shapiro, "When Charity Knows No Boundaries: Seattleites Help Syrian Refugees Here and Overseas," *Seattle Times,* May 3, 2016, www.seattletimes.com/seattle-news/northwest/seattleites-help-syrian-refugees-here-and-in-europe-i-couldnt-not-go.

151 *Their immersion began:* World Relief (www.worldrelief.org/us-offices), International Rescue Committee (www.rescue.org/who-we-are), and We Welcome Refugees (wewelcomerefugees.com) all help connect local residents with refugees in need.

9 TIME TO BEGIN

162 *For more than a year:* Learn more at questscope.org.

163 *In no time Jamie was partnered:* Learn more about GirlForward, the organization Jamie worked with, at www.girlforward.org.

the
GLOBAL
IMMERSION
project

We are a peacemaking training organization that exists to activate and resource followers of Jesus as instruments of peace.

PEACEMAKING WORKSHOPS

IMMERSION TRIPS

ECOURSES/ WEBINARS

more tools & resources available on website

· · · · · · · · · · · · · · · · · · ·

Join the everyday peacemaking movement and mend the divides in our families, communities and world.

www.globalimmerse.org